A Small History
of Political Philosophy

Victor Nuovo

Burlington, Vermont

Copyright © 2019 by Victor Nuovo

All rights reserved. No part of this publication may be reproduced, distributed, or transmitted in any form or by any means, including photocopying, recording, or other electronic or mechanical methods, without the prior written permission of the publisher, except in the case of brief quotations embodied in critical reviews and certain other noncommercial uses permitted by copyright law.

Onion River Press
191 Bank Street
Burlington, VT 05401

Publisher's Cataloging-in-Publication data
Names: Nuovo, Victor, author.
Title: A Small history of political philosophy / by Victor Nuovo.
Description: Burlington, VT: Onion River Press, 2019.
Identifiers: LCCN 2018967873 |
ISBN 978-1-949066-14-2 (pbk.) | 978-1-949066-15-9 (ebook)
Subjects: LCSH Political science—Philosophy. | Political science—Philosophy—History. | Political science—History. | BISAC PHILOSOPHY / Political
Classification: LCC JA81 .N86 2019 | DDC 320.01--dc23

Designed by The Image Farm, Middlebury, VT

Printed in the United States of America

To Betty

And these few precious days,
I'll spend with you.

Acknowledgement
And with grateful thanks to those without whose
generosity and support this book would not have been:
Angelo Lynn, Paul Ralston, Laurie Patton,
Shalom Goldman, and Sue Hoxie.

Foreword

A FRENCH MAGAZINE FROM JANUARY 2014 has been lying on our coffee table for four years. Entitled *Philosophie*, its articles feature a number of contemporary philosophers on the topic of *"Faut il s'aimer soi-meme?"* (Does one have to love oneself?) We have kept it as a token of a wonderful scholarly trip to France. But we also suspect that we have kept it because it's a symbol of what other cultures have, but America seems to struggle for—public philosophy. The term "public intellectual" is in fact borrowed from the French. In 1898 a group of prominent writers published a "Manifesto of the Intellectuals," in defense of Captain Alfred Dreyfus, a Jewish officer accused of espionage. It was their well-reasoned defense that led to Dreyfus' exoneration.

But we can travel much further back in time and space than late 19th century France for exemplary public intellectuals. As Victor Nuovo notes in these pages, Greek philosophers frequently touched upon themes of public life. In early India, public debates over the very nature of the universe were conducted between kings and priests. The loser would frequently place firewood at the feet of the winner, as a symbol and gesture of his or her servitude to the superior line of thought demonstrated by the opponent. In the early centuries of the second temple period, the Jewish court of elders, The Sanhedrin, contemplated daily matters of Jewish law and the conduct of public life. In early Chinese civilization, to philosophize was to think about the role of the ruler and the right form of government, and argue about the ruler's relationship to heaven. These were local, face-to-face debates where the nature of public life was hotly contested.

At times, philosophy was even understood as a life or death undertaking. In the early Indian texts, the Upanishads, the philosopher's head would break into a thousand pieces if his thinking proved faulty. In the early days of the Sanhedrin, to propagate thought against Jewish law was punished by death. The elders outlawed the death penalty for a *zaken mamre*—a rebellious elder—only in the first century CE. In the ancient world, philosophy was personal as well as public.

Victor Nuovo's essays in this collection are premised on another kind of life and death worry: as in the time of Plato, we are in a life and death struggle for democracy. And if we are not careful, we may lose democracy altogether. Nuovo's subjects worked during times of political crisis and social change in the West, from Plato to Spinoza to Locke to Diderot. And Nuovo's choices are deliberate; his thinkers all imply that if we do not engage in public philosophy, then the very roots of our democracy are in peril. Across the globe today, many governments are turning to embrace authoritarian rule, mounting a direct challenge to those who would defend liberal values and pluralism. Nuovo's articles also teach us that we might be well-served by adopting, and perhaps shaping for our own age, the tradition of philosophical skepticism.

It should also be noted that many of Nuovo's essays were written at a time where the study of philosophy has experienced a resurgence. An explosion in the fields of genetics and neuroscience has given rise to centers focusing on the philosophy of genetic testing and the ethics of brain surgery. As a result enrollments have increased for philosophy courses particularly dealing with bioethics.

The past two decades have witnessed a growth of centers for philosophy and public policy as the philosophical roots of our constitutional democracy are challenged and becoming frayed. As technology becomes a ubiquitous part of our daily lives, people are turning to epistemology—how we know what we know—to make sense of the brain-machine connection. As enrollments in the humanities in colleges and universities are threatened, philosophy enrollments are steady and in some places, are even rising. In other words, we need philosophy, now more than ever.

But do we only need philosophy in colleges and universities and think tanks? Nuovo's choice of publication venue states otherwise. This is another virtue of his essays: they were written for the *Addison Independent*, a well-respected local newspaper that features writers and editors who are active members of their community. Nuovo's writing assumes that there is an everyday relevance to philosophy—thinking that we can live our lives by, both publicly and privately. He assumes that the proper sphere of philosophy is as much the local newspaper as it is the local classroom. That assumption was once part of American life. The scholarly society of Phi Beta Kappa was formed in a local pub as a kind of tribute to intellectual friendship. The first American novel written by a woman, *The Gleaner*, was published in a newspaper as a serial. With the great expansion of American higher education in the second half of the 20th century, intellectual engagement became an academic endeavor, ensconced in disciplines, departments, and highly specialized journals, not in magazines and newspapers. In this way, Nuovo is going against the contemporary grain and returning us to an earlier American tradition of intellectual engagement with a wide readership.

Finally, Nuovo is taking up the challenge not only of public philosophy but also of the public sphere itself. The power of doing philosophy in a local way, and in a local venue, cannot be underestimated. The coffee shops of 18th century Enlightenment Europe played a key role in the understanding of public debate at the time and gives us a foundational image when we write about the history of the public sphere. The contemporary philosopher Jurgen Habermas saw them as the places where our contemporary idea of the public sphere was born. These coffee houses were unique places of open debate between people who knew each other—who paid each other's rent, whose children may have gone to the same school, who may have shared the same workplace.

More recent theories of the public sphere are critical of the elitist nature of these Enlightenment establishments and suggest that the contemporary obligation of participants in the public sphere should be to create more and more open spaces where more and more people can participate. We agree. What better way to do that than to publish in a local newspaper, where readers of all walks of life can engage with the arguments of the great philosophers?

In writing about philosophy and the public sphere in this way, Victor Nuovo has provided hope for the continuity of democracy itself. Perhaps we can recycle our copy of the magazine *Philosophie* after all.

Laurie Patton and Shalom Goldman

Laurie Patton is president of Middlebury College.
Shalom Goldman is the Pardon Tillinghast
Professor of Religion at Middlebury College.

Contents

Introduction	1
Thinking About Politics	4
PLATO	9
Plato's *Republic* in a Nutshell	10
Plato's Model City	14
ARISTOTLE	20
Aristotle's Political Science	21
Becoming Virtuous	25
Theory and Practice, the Great Divide	30
On Friendship, or the Tie that Binds	35
Equality and Nature	39
The City as a School of Virtue	44
MACHIAVELLI	49
Ancients and Moderns	50
Machiavelli's *The Prince*	55
Living in Dark Times with Livy	59
Machiavelli's *Discourses on Livy*	64
HOBBES	69
Thomas Hobbes, our Contemporary	70
Hobbes' Politics	74
Lingering Problems with Hobbes	79
Hobbes on Religion	84

SPINOZA	89
Spinoza on Free Inquiry	90
How to Read the Bible (According to Spinoza)	94
Spinoza's Politics	99
JOHN LOCKE	105
Introducing John Locke	106
Does the Mind Always Think?	110
Locke Against Patriarchy	114
The Origin of Civil Society	119
Private Property	124
Liberalism and the Meaning of History	129
DIDEROT	134
Diderot's Political Naturalism	135
Diderot on Duty and Justice	140
Diderot's Religion	145
THE AMERICANS	150
Establishing the Rule of Law	151
Power to "The People"	156
The Reasonableness of the Constitution	161
The Irony of American History	166
…	171
Suggestions for Further Reading	172
About the Author	173

Introduction

THE ESSAYS THAT FOLLOW were first published in the Addison Independent, where they appeared serially. Many readers expressed a desire to have them all together in one place so that they might more easily be read and compared. They are now presented here as a connected set, meant to unfold the history of western political thought.

I wrote these essays to satisfy a deep-felt need. Politics is all about the corporate use of power for peaceful ends. This power has no limits unless regulated by the rule of law, which in turn depends upon the good will and right understanding of those who govern and the people whom they govern. Politics is an art, shaped by a knowledge and understanding of its traditions. Where such understanding is lacking, our path becomes dysfunctional and dangerous. I perceived a lack of it today, and therefore began to search for the foundations of wisdom in the European tradition of political thought from antiquity to the modern era.

What is offered in the pages that follow is but a small portion of this tradition. Yet I believe that the philosophers whose thought is presented here have touched upon most if not all of the major themes of political thought: the use and abuse of corporate human power; the means of creating and sustaining a civil society that will promote the one and avoid the other; and, above all, what it means to be human. It is noteworthy that these thinkers lived and wrote during times of political crisis and social change. Practical necessity made them philosophers. All were sober realists, skeptical of human aspirations and doubtful about human progress. They recognized that politics filled an essential need, to regulate human life, to pacify human motives, and to restrain our worst passions. They realized that government, when faithful to its purpose, can achieve these ends, even in the worst of times.

My subjects will be eminent political philosophers, ancient and modern, among them Plato, Aristotle, Machiavelli, Hobbes, Spinoza, Locke, and Diderot. Their writings influenced the framers of the US Constitution: Alexander Hamilton, John Jay, and James Madison, as they endeavored to create and perpetuate the American Republic, and it is with them, original political thinkers in their own right, that the series will conclude.

Plato, who comes first, lived during the death throes of Athenian democracy. His writings may be read as commentaries on his times. They are, to be sure, philosophical discourses, and they raise many enduring problems, like, What is knowledge? What is beauty? What is the motivation to be just? Can a civil society be sustained pure and inviolable? But his aim is never merely theoretical; nor is it merely practical. His writings are reflective, self-examining, and composed with an art that captivates the mind and never lets go. One never tires of Plato and never stops learning from him. What impresses me most is the brooding pessimism that pervades his thought, poignantly expressed in everything that he has written, a darkness that makes all the brighter the splendid abstractions of beauty and goodness that fill the horizon of his thought. But this is all background to his political vision to which one could devote a lifetime.

Now, some say we are witnessing the death throes of American democracy, and that our nation is doomed to suffer the fate of Athens: a perversion of popular democracy into tyranny. Surely these are trying times. But if Plato witnessed similar troubles, it may be said that James Madison and the framers of the Constitution, with whom this series concludes, anticipated them, and devised a system of political order well-suited to our mixed nature, of good and evil. It is my hope, then, that these essays may be read and reflected upon and that the wisdom of the eminent thinkers presented in them will serve to guide us and keep us on a steady course.

⁂

Victor Nuovo

Middlebury, Vermont
November 2018

Thinking About Politics

Our nation has reached a critical moment in its history. Its people are divided into ideological warring camps; our constitutional system, designed to negotiate differences, seems no longer effective; our culture has become grossly narcissistic; self-pity has emerged as our chief virtue, and overall, there seems to be a lack of proper understanding if not ignorance of the tradition of the rule of law, on which the survival of our nation depends. Surely, we live in a time of troubles.

Our institutions and practices are not self-perpetuating; they require a constant infusion of thought and commitment. The framers of our constitution could not have foreseen what has happened today, but they anticipated it and provided a remedy for it in our founding documents. The task now falls upon us as citizens to study these documents and recover the ideas and principles of our republic presented there, to think them through, to rededicate ourselves to them, and to apply them anew. These ideas and principles are part of an intellectual heritage that is ancient. Merely to rededicate ourselves to them is not enough. We must first understand them and the heritage that has formed them. We must begin at the beginning.

I begin with Plato and Aristotle. Plato (427–347 BCE) is the founder of political philosophy in the European tradition. Aristotle (384–322 BCE) erected the superstructure. He invented the academic discipline of political science, gave it its name, clarified its themes, and endowed it with concepts and terms that have become the alphabet of political thinking. Together they bequeathed to posterity, to us, the very idea of Constitutionalism upon which our nation is founded: the idea that the authority of government arises from and is determined by fundamental law, and that all citizens, in every walk of life, public and private, are subject to this law and obligated to be its keepers. A fundamental law is like the foundation of a house: allow it to decay or otherwise hinder its use, and the house will collapse.

Plato and Aristotle overlap. Aristotle spent twenty years in Plato's Academy. He entered as a youth, and left as an adult, a mature philosopher with plans to begin his own school. During these two decades, Plato's last years, Plato was at work rethinking political theory and composing his final work, *The Laws*. It has become a classic of political philosophy; its central themes are constitutionalism and the rule of law. Aristotle comments on *The Laws* and the *Republic*, in his *Politics*, which is also regarded as a classic and an essential work on constitutional theory. His comments are especially valuable, because of his close contact with Plato, as his student, and, later, as his colleague. What Aristotle learned he revised and refashioned to fit his own insights and purposes.

It is noteworthy for us that Plato and Aristotle had a very special object in mind when they engaged in political thinking. It was the *polis*, the ancient Greek city. The polis was, in their thought, supposed to be autonomous, sovereign, and self-sufficient. The term is usually translated "city-state" to distinguish it from the modern "nation-state". In size, situation, and mode of government, the Greek *polis* is like a Vermont town. It is their direct ancestor. Our towns lack sovereignty and have limited autonomy, yet they are an enduring testimony to the importance of local government and the opportunities that government provides us to exercise our franchise as citizens.

The ancient *polis* was a vibrant center of political and social life: not only was it sovereign and autonomous, its legislative scope was all-comprehending, encompassing public safety, health, and welfare; commerce, education, and religion; foreign relations, defense, and the moral life. The centrality of the *polis* in Greek political thought is evident in their key terms: *politeia* signified the art of governing, as well as a city's constitution or fundamental law, or more generally political theory; a *polites* was a citizen; a *politikos* was a public official or statesman. Our terms "politics" and "politician" retain the sounds but have lost much of the meaning. The same may be said of the term "citizen", which is derived from the Latin *civis* and *civitas*.

During the lifetimes of Plato and Aristotle, the Greek *polis* became an endangered species. Plato blamed this on commerce and expansion through colonization, which caused rivalry and wars between cities, and a chronic contest for hegemony among them, evoking fantasies of empire, greed, and vain ambition. During Plato's lifetime, the sovereignty of the *polis* was in doubt; during Aristotle's lifetime, its fate was decided.

Aristotle was born in Stagira, a minor city in northeastern Greece bordering Macedonia. His father was a physician who served for a time as court physician to Amyntas III, king of Macedon. When he was seventeen, Aristotle went to Athens to study in Plato's Academy and remained there for twenty years, until Plato's death, in 347. Displeased by Plato's successor, he left the Academy and Athens to seek his fortune elsewhere. Four years later, Philip II of Macedon, Amyntas' successor, summoned Aristotle to tutor his son Alexander. Philip had become master of Greece and was instrumental in ending the era of free and independent cities. Alexander succeeded him. He endeavored to conquer the whole world and might have succeeded, had he lived longer—he was not yet thirty-two when he died. Yet history has accorded him the eponym "the Great", while historians use the year of his death, 323 BCE, to mark the end of the Classical era and the beginning of the so-called Hellenistic age. The name "Hellenistic" is significant. Aristotle taught Alexander well, for the pupil turned out to be not only an adventurer, who wanted to conquer the world, but a cultural-nationalist who desired to make the nations he conquered Greek, to Hellenize them.

Since the Greeks called their homeland Hellas, the Greek verb *hellenizein* means to cause someone to speak Greek and to adopt Greek customs and manners. During the Hellenistic age, the power of Greek cities declined even as new cities were founded; the field of politics was fertile for imperialist adventurers like Alexander, and the seedbed for Rome, whose era followed. When Rome achieved supreme power, its elite prided themselves on the fact that they were fluent in Greek and had studied in Athens, much like elitists of my generation who prided themselves on being fluent in French and having studied at the Sorbonne. The Greek *polis* and Athens in particular became emblems of past glory and icons of cultural elitism. Aristotle not only lived through this change but helped shape it.

Postscript:

Readers who enjoy visualizing the time and place of great personages should view Raphael's fresco, *The School of Athens*, which can be accessed online.

PLATO

Plato's *Republic* in a Nutshell

Plato wrote the *Republic* to give expression to an ideal of a city in which a perfect justice has been established in all of its parts. He was not naive. He did not suppose that his ideal city could be easily realized, if at all; in the end he concluded that it could not. Yet his pessimism never led him to conclude that the ideal was false; rather, he concluded that everyday reality was false, a mere shadow. Thus, the idea of justice, which is the central theme of the *Republic*, represented to him a transcendent value, accessible to thought and to those few who looked beyond the ordinary and everyday world; these few he called philosophers.

Justice is a moral virtue, a ruling characteristic of a life well-lived. Plato supposed that there are four cardinal virtues essential to being good: courage, temperance, prudence, and justice—he occasionally added others, such as a quick wit, good memory, and greatness of soul or magnificence, which is the ability to imagine and achieve great things beyond the merely personal or parochial. Justice, however, is supreme among the virtues. One may be brave, temperate, prudent, and uniquely gifted and still live an immoral life. Indeed, without justice, these qualities merely enhance corruption. Justice makes the difference: it encompasses all the other virtues and outstanding qualities and endows them with a special quality that justice uniquely exemplifies, without which nothing can have moral value.

What is justice? It is the ruling virtue of civil society and the individual soul, of the city and its government. Among the key features of justice is that it does no harm: conflicts are mediated; punishment is restorative, never vengeful. Justice is also tolerant and impartial; differences in gender identity and sexual preference make no political or moral difference; the aim of a just government is to foster gainful and useful employment for all its inhabitants and the material means to subsist and to flourish; free education for all, from pre-natal care through higher education. There is an equitable redistribution of excess wealth. Justice is always impartial and equitably maintained.

To achieve these ends is the duty of those who govern. Much of the *Republic* is devoted to their education. The rulers and guardians of a city must be persons, male or female, who are gifted; capable of self-mastery; indifferent to their own personal interests; indifferent to personal fame and fortune or any other variety of personal gain, even reputation; who are perfectly selfless, caring only for the welfare of the people whom they have been trained to govern and protect—never desiring a reward or approval or praise for their accomplishments. Such ideally minded persons will prove so constant in securing the good of the governed that they are taken for granted or even despised. And yet they bear all with equanimity and grace. Justice is the quality that makes them so; it is the form of their lives and the essence of all they do. Some commentators have even noted a similarity between Plato's just ruler and the suffering servant: "he was despised and rejected by men; a man of sorrows and acquainted with grief, and as one from whom men hide their faces, he was despised, and we esteemed him not. Surely he has born our griefs…" (Isaiah 53:3–4).

If Plato is right about justice, one wonders why anyone would choose to be a just ruler? And if the task of just rulers is to create a truly just society, why would anyone want to be a part of it, since the selfish question "what's in it for me" must always have a negative answer? Nevertheless, Plato was sure that such a society is the only way to secure lasting happiness; only the just can be happy. Seeking one's own advantage before all else only causes misery to oneself most of all.

Plato's defense of this claim is related to his admittedly paradoxical belief that only philosophers should rule. He is not referring to the ordinary run-of-the-mill philosopher. He meant someone who has persisted in philosophical inquiry to its ultimate goal and glimpsed Being itself, which he equated with the very Idea of Goodness—not a mere abstraction, but something endowed with power, the cause of existence. He believed that truth of this sort is not arrived at by an empirical method, or by experiment and induction, but by purely intellectual or logical pursuits. The mind ascends to truth through a play of concepts, an ascent marked by a degrading of the particular and material. He called his method "dialectic", whereby the mind leaves behind the everyday world of sensory experience; once in the realm of forms or ideas, it contemplates the archetypes of every being, chief among them forms of pure value, such as Justice itself, Beauty itself, and, finally, the Good all by itself, radiant, pure, infinitely vital, and captivating.

These are not mere abstractions, but potent realities and inexhaustible causes of being; merely to contemplate them brings immeasurable joy without end, in contrast to which all other pleasures and delights are mere infatuations, passing fancies. Plato was the first and perhaps the only genuine transcendentalist, yet true philosophers, knowing what justice is, are not allowed to continue to dwell in this paradise of forms. Guided by the very idea of justice, they regard it as a duty to descend to the world of appearances and counterfeits, to fill the role of philosopher king.

In this respect, Plato's *Republic* is a manifesto for elitism. The elite are persons perfected by justice, whose judgment is determined by truth, and whose moral nature assures that they always do the right thing. A city ruled and protected by such paragons of justice hardly requires laws; if any are needed, the good judgment of the ruler will provide them and ensure that they are fit to promote virtue in the city. Such is the ideal city that Plato envisions, but being an ideal, never to be perfectly realized, it evokes a mood of deep pessimism. Human frailty, fallibility, and downright corruption are the reason for this: self-serving nastiness and backbiting of political rivals, the phony populist rhetoric of self-promoters, and the fickleness and selfishness of the people, the *hoi polloi*. Just as the nobility of impartial justice filled Plato's mind with joy, so the political realities of Athens made him despair that true justice could ever be achieved. He concludes the *Republic* not with a paean of praise but a narrative of death and rebirth, a hypothesis of the migration of souls, along with a faint promise of deliverance.

In the *Laws*, Plato is in search of a plausible alternative to the rule of the just; a model city that exemplifies the rule of law, and which approximates justice, but may sometimes be unjust, and in any case ambiguous. His depiction of the model city launched the political practice of constitutionalism.

Plato's Model City

IMAGINE MIDDLEBURY AS PLATO'S MODEL CITY—the model city, which was his practical solution to implementing the rule of law. This is not so fanciful, for the Greek *polis* is the direct ancestor of the Vermont town. Plato imagined his model city as inhabited by five thousand families or homesteads in a territory the size of Addison County, a place well-endowed with water and timber and fertile soil, the essential resources. Our system of government and Plato's are virtually the same: an elected council whose head is first among equals, along with a public assembly, a charter or constitution, and the rule of law. And although Middlebury is not, like the Greek *polis*, a sovereign state, it is the shire town of Addison County, and its vibrant urban center reflects this fact. All our needs and entertainments are provided in Middlebury: we have markets, a parent-child center, schools from kindergarten through college, libraries, a theatre, a hospital, and the means of public safety. It is possible to live one's whole life here and be satisfied.

These considerations should provide us with a sense of familiarity, if not empathy, when we consider this ideal central to Plato's thought and allow us to understand better the purposes of its institutions and how they might apply to us.

The first requisite of the model city is the rule of law. It must be a fundamental law whose primary purpose is to enable the city to be as self-perpetuating as possible; in short, a constitution that prescribes a political system that preserves itself and whose use is self-renewing. It must be a law whose goal is the good of the whole: peace, stability, order, and an equitable or livable share in the common wealth for all who reside in it. Or as our own constitution puts it, a "perfect union", one that is tranquil, secure against enemies, and geared toward the public welfare, while securing the blessings of liberty for all, which is just. In contrast, a law that allows the winners of popular elections to take all, to refashion the city to suit their likes and dislikes, would not serve it well; it would cause resentments, jealousies, increasing instability, and even civil war.

Plato offers a measured endorsement of liberty in *Laws*. He proposes a mixed constitution: one that balances executive authority against popular opinion, anticipating the arguments for a separation of powers that James Madison made in *The Federalist Papers*. In other words, the legal framework envisioned by Plato was meant to preserve liberty as regulated by unity and wisdom.

Plato's model city must be well-situated geographically, accessible to its outlying districts, yet not so accessible to the world as to be easy prey to pirates and predatory raiders. Therefore, it should be located away from the sea and great navigable rivers. This provision was also meant to guard against the enemy within: Plato feared that commerce, excessive economic growth, the accumulation of vast fortunes, and luxurious living by a privileged elite would prove inevitable sources of corruption. To prevent this, he prescribed that family fortunes must not rise above a certain level, and, if they did, the excess should be redistributed; there would be neither poverty nor wealth out of all proportion in the model city. Every household would be given possession of a portion of land sufficient to their well-being, if properly cultivated; it would belong to them and their heirs inalienably.

In this respect, Plato desired that his model city would be as near as possible to a natural being. Its flourishing would be like the flourishing of a tree or a rose bush, and although Plato did express the hope that a city if modeled correctly might "last for all time", he did not suppose it had the quality of eternity, but of a durable constitution; its chief goal is not expansion, but regeneration. The model city would have a military force, but only for purposes of self-defense. And because its mode of life is neither luxurious nor extravagant it would be less likely to become the victim of predatory adventurers. Its people, and especially its rulers, would eschew all aspirations to glory. It would have no ambition to grow beyond its own borders, no dreams of empire, and no grand narrative of manifest destiny. Hence, it would have no history. The model city would be as much a part of nature as its citizens can make it.

Consistent with Plato's economic policies, citizens of the model city would practice no trade. The arts and crafts, including medicine, would be performed by resident aliens and in some instances by slaves. Plato did not consider slavery to be unnatural; nor did he find it necessary to justify the holding of slaves. Slaves were needed to work the land and perform the functions of household servants. In contrast, citizenship would come with being born into a landed family, making citizens a landed gentry. Besides the management of their property, citizens would be eligible to serve as officers of government or in the military. This applied to women as well as men. In the *Republic*, Plato affirmed the equality of women, a goal he meant to achieve by doing away with traditional family customs. As well, he advocated free love and raising children in common. In *Laws*, his later text, the family is restored, but Plato remained nevertheless convinced about women's equality and their right to education and to participate in government.

Laws are duties that citizens owe to each other and to others who reside or have business within the city. And there must be a reason or beneficial purpose to every law. Much like a physician who, when prescribing treatment to a patient, explains how it will serve to restore or maintain good health, so a lawgiver must explain in good faith how a proposed law benefits the citizens, civil society, and overall the public good.

Especially noteworthy are the model city's practices in punishing criminals. As in the *Republic*, Plato advocated a policy of restorative justice premised on the belief that every person is a rational being and that criminals can be reasoned with. Plato did not suppose human beings are by nature good, only that they can learn from experience. Prisons, then, are not places of punishment, or mere sites of confinement, but counseling centers or schools of virtue. The rehabilitative process must be conducted with the greatest patience. When after repeated efforts an offender seems incorrigible, Plato prescribed capital punishment executed quietly in a place remote from the public square.

It should be clear that Plato was no advocate of globalism. Nonetheless, he considered an acquaintance with the practices and policies of foreign cities useful, if not necessary. A city must not stagnate, but must learn new things in law and technology that might improve the quality of life for all residents; a city must not only be self-sufficient but also worldly wise. While foreign travel was restricted, travelers would be interviewed on their return by the Council to learn what they learned. The wisest of these travelers would be made members of the Nocturnal Council, a body of citizens experienced in practice and demonstrably wise, who would meet regularly to discuss laws and legal theory. This council was to function as a living intelligence of the city; neither legislators nor rulers, but teachers and regulators insofar as their wisdom and good judgment infused every other operation of government.

Postscript:

I can think of no philosophical work that better fits an environmental agenda than Plato's *Laws*, most especially the idea of a city as a living thing that endures by self-regeneration. Whether overall the city imagined by Plato would be truly just is doubtful, for with citizens as slaveholders, it does not provide for a true equality. Nevertheless, there is much in the constitution of the model city that is worth considering

ARISTOTLE

Aristotle's Political Science

Now we come to Aristotle. He was the parent not only of political science but of logic, physics, biology, psychology, rhetoric, poetics, metaphysics, and, generally, the theory of scientific method and explanation. He was the first to codify concepts and distinctions that appear commonplace not only in theoretical discourse but also in everyday conversation. Distinctions between theory and practice, to begin with, as well as those between form and content, subject and predicate, cause and effect, essence and attribute, potentiality and actuality, and necessity and contingency. As well, he outlined basic concepts like method in science, in addition to various ideas of causality: material, efficient, formal, and final. There is more: he also originated literary concepts such as mimesis (imitation), plot, character, catharsis, and recognition. And finally he perfected the practice of abstraction, or forming abstract ideas and the universal terms that denote them, of which I will soon give an example. It is in this last practice that he differs most from Plato.

The rediscovery of his writings during the late Middle Ages caused a renewal of learning predating the Renaissance. His ideas inspired the founding of universities in Europe, outfitting them with a ready-made curriculum and a model for the university lecture that is still in use today. No wonder then that he was reverently referred to as "the master of those who know". I remember as a student in my first graduate seminar being told that we are all Aristotelians without knowing it, because many of his concepts and terms and methods of inquiry have become common sense or, at least, common discourse. If this is true—and it seems to me true enough—then we must not ignore Aristotle. At the very least, reading him will enable us to recover the meanings of words we use every day with only a passive understanding, if that, of what they mean.

It is true that, with the passage of time, Aristotle's stature in the pantheon of great thinkers has diminished. His ideas appear to us now mere commonplaces and consequently degraded; there is an aspect of obsolescence about them, especially in logic and physics. A measure of this is true of his political thinking also, but only a small measure. Aristotle was completely absorbed in his time and place. He was a proud Greek, an elitist, a male chauvinist, notwithstanding that he did not cut a very impressive masculine figure—he had spindly legs, beady eyes, and overall is said to have been unhandsome; like Plato, he was an apologist of slavery, but he parted ways from his master in being a denier of women's rights, and a sentimentalist with regard to the golden age of Greece when its cities were free and independent. There is poignancy in Aristotle's pride, for he lived just at the moment of profound political upheaval, when Greek cities were fighting a losing battle to maintain a measure of their independence and cultural authenticity. He was not only an eye-witness in these affairs but a participant in them as well.

Aristotle's theory of politics consists of two parts, which have come down to us in separate works entitled *Ethics* and *Politics*. Keep in mind that he regarded ethics as an integral part of political science. Nowadays, they are treated separately in college curricula, taught by separate departments. Of course, college curricula are expressions of modern culture, which regards the person as morally separable from society, perfectible in isolation from it. Aristotle would have found such an idea puzzling, if not lamentable. To his view, we are political animals first and foremost. The perfection of human life is unrealizable apart from the city; a life that can be perfected only in a city, or not at all.

Hence, he opens his discourse on ethics by introducing the idea of political science with a grand generalization: "Every art, every science, every action, every act of choice [that is, everything we do or contemplate doing!] aims at some good; hence it has been well said that the Good is the end towards which all things aim". It is a wonderfully crafted sentence, a Platonic bubble, which he bursts in the very next: "But it appears that these ends differ". Which is to say, "Good" is a mere abstraction, a general term that has a variety of different meanings depending on the context in which it is used.

Still, Aristotle finds a way to combine all these ends in a single place. All pursuits of the "Good" occur in a city, the activities of a civilized people. Hence, there is indeed a Supreme Good—not an idea, as Plato supposed, but a place, the *polis*, and the science that unites them in thought is political science. The highest human good is a well-governed city consisting of responsible or virtuous citizens, where creativity flourishes, and a happy life can be lived in a variety of ways. In this respect, Aristotle's idea of ethics is wholly secular. The good life, morally and happily, is essentially a political life. This does not mean that Aristotle was irreligious, only that he regarded religion as a subordinate part of politics. He was a proponent of secular religion.

Ethics is the theory of human flourishing, of life well-lived, of human existence endowed with civility. Civility is not a natural endowment; rather, it is achieved through training and perfected by regular self-discipline; in an active life directed not by the prods of conscience but by the agile direction of a rational mind open to possibilities. A large part of the *Ethics* is devoted to a description of this training and discipline, which is properly regarded as training-in-citizenship. (The basics of Aristotle's method will be the subject of my next essay). There is more: Aristotle also gives instruction on how to be wise, in the best practical sense of making wise choices; and he wrote a most insightful and definitive account of friendship as a social bond. The *Ethics* concludes with an examination of the nature of happiness. His work, designed as a handbook for citizens, is still useful today.

Postscript:

Aristotle's major work on ethics is entitled *Nichomachean Ethics* (it was supposedly addressed to his son Nichomachus) but is most often referred to simply as *Ethics*. His major work on politics is entitled just that, *Politics*. It is a sequel to *Ethics*. Both are available in reliable translations in Oxford World Classics.

Becoming Virtuous

ACCORDING TO ARISTOTLE, A VIRTUE is a behavioral habit that is acquired by practice. Becoming virtuous is no different from becoming skilled in an art or craft or sport. It requires experience and instruction and the use of reason, good judgment, and a wealth of experience.

Aristotle uses the term "habit" to describe a disposition to act in a certain way; he adds reason and judgment to emphasize that virtuous actions are always deliberate, suited to the occasion, and measured. A virtue is a habit that we and others can count on; it makes our mutual dealings civil.

Aristotle describes a virtue as a mean between two extremes, the one involving excess, the other deficiency. For example, courage is a mean between recklessness and cowardliness; temperance is the mean between debauchery and neurasthenia; generosity, a mean between extravagance and miserliness; pride, a mean between vanity and humility; and good temper, a mean between irascibility and indifference that couldn't care less. There are more, to be sure. Reason and judgment are applied when steering a course between these extremes, and the more experience we acquire in our efforts—the more observant we are of the behavior of ourselves and others—the more skilled we become in virtue, the better at avoiding extremes. Aristotle calls this capacity right reason or thinking correctly.

All of these are social virtues. To acquire them, Aristotle believed, it was necessary to be with others, to belong in a society situated in a place: for example, courage manifests in the defense of one's homeland; temperance in regulating one's public and private passions; generosity in sharing one's wealth; and pride in seeking to accomplish great things that benefit others.

The simplicity of the method belies the difficulty of applying it. Aristotle regards embodying virtue as a continual experiment in living. Every judgment is different, drawn from different circumstances, so that finding the mean is different every time—always a new discovery, a new instance of right reason. For a tried and experienced person, the challenge to evaluate different circumstances brings satisfaction; it is the seasoning of an active life.

Consider the virtue of temperance. It involves regulating one's temper or keeping it under control. It is an important civic virtue; Aristotle calls it 'gentility.' In public discourse about critical issues, passion often prevails over reason. And yet all would agree that reason or rational judgment, a careful weighing of principles and consequences, ought to decide what is the right or best thing to do. For passions are blind.

Yet in the public sphere, mere reason lacks persuasive force. In contrast, passion persuades or compels but does not instruct. A virtuous politician must seek a position in between cool rationality and passion, for the goal of political discourse, morally conceived, is informed consent from the citizenry sustained by commitment—commitment which is itself a virtue that steers a course between blind adherence and absolute indifference. It takes training and experience to achieve this goal; as Aristotle describes it, it involves a readiness to become angry "for such causes and for such a length of time as principle may require". In such instances, the anger is real and heartfelt, but the action that the anger impels is reasonable and fair.

To look at another example, justice is also an important civic virtue. Unlike Plato, and more like us, Aristotle regards justice as an abstract term with different uses or meanings. We use it to signify the practice of fairness or equity in all our dealings, or in acting lawfully. Injustice, on the other hand, signifies the practice of willfully disregarding for law, caring only about oneself, or getting as much as one can for oneself. Laws, like people, also can be just or unjust; laws that favor a privileged minority, or that give special advantage to the party that happens to be in power, are unjust. Just laws aim at the welfare and happiness of all. In this respect, principled disobedience to unjust laws *is* just. We know this as civil disobedience, an honorable tradition. But we must never forget that it is a practice which also requires an abiding respect for law. Civil disobedience is an endeavor to make laws just, not an effort to do away with the rule of law. In contrast, the current paranoia against law and government that has raised its ugly head in our time even in the highest places is a perfect instance of injustice, vile and reprehensible. Such abhorrence of the rule of law is motivated by narcissism, resentment, and vicious self-interest.

Now, even though virtue takes root as a set of rational states or dispositions, Aristotle believed that it is founded and sustained by passions. Two in particular: honor and shame. The honorable, together with the good, are the ideals of Greek culture. For Aristotle, the good is the general name for whatever is beneficial or promotes enduring happiness in human life. The honorable, or noble, requires more effort to understand; the Greek word *kalon*, meaning noble, is more often translated as "beauty".

Perhaps if we fix in our minds the figures of Greek sculpture, figures finely wrought and full of grace, we can begin to understand how ideas of what is beautiful and what is honorable might converge in a single sentiment. Aristotle associates the noble with heroic action. Heroes are motivated by a sense of honor when they enter into battle; it is front and center in the motto of the United States Military Academy, memorialized by the farewell address General MacArthur gave there: "Duty, Honor, Country". The practice of honorable, or noble, action applies to all of the virtues. A virtuous life is a noble life. In his use of this idea, Aristotle seems to rely on his mentor Plato, whose idea of a just ruler is of one whose life is wholly dedicated to the welfare of others and whose duty is to serve without any regard to personal gain. Nobility indeed.

Shame is another social passion, the reverse side to honor in motivating the attainment of virtue. I am reminded of the scene when Adam and Eve, having eaten of the forbidden fruit of the Tree of the Knowledge of Good and Evil, stand naked and ashamed. Their shame was a fear of discovery, signaling their guilt but also their awareness of their nakedness (Genesis 3: 7–11). It is a curious comment on the discovery of sexuality, perhaps, and of a loss of innocence. How they are connected, the narrator of the Old Testament does not say.

Yet the Greek idea of shame is nobler than this. The sense of shame as a motive of virtue indicates a fear of discovery:

not just of being found out by others but of self-discovery, of recognizing one's own shortcomings. Shame is the realization by an individual that he or she does not measure up to a noble ideal. It is a sense of one's moral nakedness. Such a sensibility may be absent from us moderns; if so, it is our loss. Perhaps it is not an irrecoverable loss.

Theory and Practice, the Great Divide

AMONG THE TOPICS that Aristotle treats in the *Ethics* are the intellectual virtues, or capacities of mind that individuals must cultivate in order to become good citizens. Aristotle lists five of them: knowledge, art, prudence, wisdom, and understanding. It is a curious combination of the practical and the theoretical, of theory and practice.

"Knowledge and art" are more or less equivalent to "science and technology". Knowledge is the perception of how things are, of truth or reality. The term Aristotle uses is *episteme*. The philosophical discipline "epistemology" consists of inquiries into the theory of knowledge; that is, how we know anything, and the difference between knowledge and belief. What Aristotle meant by this term is not occasional knowledge, such as how many toes there are on my foot, or teeth in my mouth (which, I confess, I don't know, never having counted them, and I hesitate to do so now, at my age), but a well-established kind of knowledge, supported by evidence gathered from systematic observation, and by precise definition. In short, science. Counting is perhaps the most basic activity of science and provides the greatest certainty, well illustrating what Aristotle meant by science. If I count the fingers on my hands and the toes on my feet, I can say with certainty that I have exactly the same number of toes as fingers. And I can generalize, after systematic observation, that the same is true of most human animals, which leads into observations about the regularities of nature, and more deeply into their causes and statistical reliability. Aristotle was not so very well versed in mathematics, and statistics had not yet been invented, but he appreciated the utility of arithmetic as an example of the perfection of knowledge; and in his notion of a perfect science he anticipated Euclid, who rose to eminence not long after Aristotle's death.

Knowledge involves a certainty of truth, of the way things are. I have already mentioned the distinction between knowledge and belief; what one *knows* is certain and true, whereas what one *believes* may be false. Therefore, however ardently we may cling to them, beliefs remain uncertain without conclusive evidence, which may never prove forthcoming. It is essential to distinguish between knowledge and belief correctly. Needless to say, Aristotle would look askance at anyone who seemed content to be a person of faith.

Aristotle's term for art is *techne*, whence our term, technology. *Techne* signifies a refined practice whose purpose is to make useful things, things that benefit us in life, and enhance the art of living. Success in this endeavor requires knowing how things are: the nature of the materials we employ and the conditions that apply in joining them together. The motto of the DuPont Corporation, "better things for better living through chemistry" captures this well enough. Aristotle's idea of art is much broader, however. It includes the art of speech, poetry, architecture, painting, and sculpture, but in all these instances, the method is generally the same. For him, the purpose of any practical art is social enhancement. He did not envision modern technology, but given his dislike of any excess, especially excess wealth, he probably would have been troubled by the great power technology has unleashed, exceeding the limits of prudent use.

Prudence—the Greek term is *phronesis*—is good sense or, as the term is often translated, practical wisdom in contrast to the theoretical sort, which I will get to shortly. It is an ability to decide as occasion requires what appears to be the best or most advantageous thing to do; it is good judgment, which depends upon experience and a willingness to learn from what one experiences. At its best, prudence is rational and deliberative, a careful weighing of pro and con between various strategies and methods to achieve desired ends, then choosing what seems the best way to go. The opposite of prudence is folly.

But prudence is never certain; it depends more on belief than knowledge. Here is the great divide between theory and practice. Good judgments often fail. So, the bedrock principle of practical wisdom is that things can always go wrong, very wrong, as the poet Robert Burns put it when speaking to a mouse:

> But Mousie, thou art no thy lane [you are not alone],
> In proving foresight may be vain;
> The best-laid schemes o' mice an' men
> Gang aft agley [often go awry],
> An' lea'e us nought but grief an' pain,
> For promis'd joy!

In future ages, philosophers would come to regard prudence as the art of discerning the probable, and counsel that probability can function as the guide of life. But this is an idea that Aristotle lacked.

Although an empiricist, Aristotle preferred the theoretical sciences, and therefore his account of the intellectual virtues culminated in wisdom, which he equates with pure understanding. The Greek term he uses is *nous*, or intellect. We use the term "intellection" to represent an ultimate state of knowledge whereby one understands something perfectly and completely. Ultimate in the sense that no further inquiry is needed, because there is nothing more to know, every wrinkle ironed out. The object of knowledge is there fully revealed before the gaze of the intellect. Such perfect knowledge is not only complete but also enduring and everlasting—the pleasure of contemplation mimics the mind of the creator. It was this sort of intelligence that Aristotle supposed was the cause of existence, what he described as eternal and uncaused intellection of the whole of reality. It is this intellection whose perfection, he thought, the physical world imitates, although never with complete success. Aristotle called such intellect the unmoved mover, a state that all beings desire. The motivation to achieve it is what makes the world turn and activates everything within the world.

In light of this, Aristotle came to an understanding of what he took to be the whole of reality. The virtuous life, one of constant and diligent self-discipline and of deliberate action, achieves its end in wisdom and understanding, and in the contemplation of truth, which is sufficient compensation for all the uncertainties of everyday life. Centuries later, Spinoza would take Aristotle's thought and shape it into a philosophical system.

But were they right? I conclude this essay with some questions. How far must we go in our understanding of the nature of things to be secure in our moral and political understanding? And must we be assured that by living morally and politically just lives, we will receive some transcendent reward? Must practical wisdom be merely preparatory to a supreme wisdom, or should we be satisfied with an ordinary life among mice and men?

On Friendship, or the Tie that Binds

ARISTOTLE SUGGESTS THAT LOVE or a feeling of mutual affection between citizens may be a more effective means of unifying a city than justice—indeed that the latter may depend upon the former. It is an alluring thought and deserves to be explored.

He observes that there are three kinds of friendship; one founded on mutual utility, another on mutual pleasure, and a third that he designates perfect friendship. Almost as an afterthought, he arrives at friendliness, which is a civic virtue rather than a private relation with some person. Yet, of all the varieties of friendship, it is best of all.

First, there is friendship based on utility: I know a man who has the remarkable ability to fix any household appliance that breaks down and whom I can rely upon to come to my aid whenever I need him, even on weekends. He asks only a modest return for his services, far less than he deserves, which causes me to hold him in the highest regard. But is he my friend? There is a relationship of mutuality between us inasmuch as I desire him to prosper and so am quick to pay him and recommend him to others. His readiness to serve may be based on the pleasure he takes in fixing things and in solving mechanical problems that the engineers who designed the appliances in question never imagined could happen. But, I find in his attitude something more, a desire to use his skills to help others, which I take to be a kind of affection or friendliness, directed not to any one person in particular, but to anyone in our community who requires his services. And I feel towards him not only gratitude, but a wish that he receive the best in life. So, to answer my question: Yes, he is a friend, but this is because of his friendliness and the gratitude it evokes. Our friendship is one based on utility and respect, and not on intimacy and affection.

Aristotle's second category of friendships are those based on mutual pleasure, the pleasure of company or companionship; associations of persons drawn together by elective affinities, who are kindred spirits. These arise between individuals more or less in regular contact. But they need not—these sorts of friendships may be casual and commonplace: a clerk in a local shop who always has some kind words to say, or who is witty, with whom one can share items of mutual interest, such as sports, movies, or daily observations. We all have many friends of this sort. Without them, everyday life would not be worth living; our daily commerce with each other would be grim and, well, unfriendly.

Aristotle regards these first two sorts of friendship as deficient, for the whole moral person is lacking in them. Perfect friendship, then, is a mutual relationship of love between two individuals, where each party unselfishly desires what is best for the other—a desire motivated by pure goodness, or the wish to realize something unconditionally good not for oneself but for another. It follows that perfect friendship is a relationship of complete equality, and to be realized, we might believe, it requires that two persons live together, as in marriage. However, Aristotle supposed that this sort of friendship can occur *only* between two good men of equal social status, allowing that it may also involve sexual intimacy. Because he could not conceive of marriage as other than a relationship between a man and a woman, wherein men take wives as servants and homemakers, he did not regard marriage as friendship—even if, at its best, it would involve a natural affection between man and wife. In this view, Aristotle was mistaken, as we have now come to see that marriage is in fact just such a relationship of perfect mutuality between two persons, any two persons, whatever their gender or sexual preference or race or ethnicity.

Aristotle also supposed that friendship is more likely to occur between two men of the same race. As a statement of probability, this may have a small measure of truth in it. But as a moral statement, it is false. Affinity only toward one's own race would deprive friendship of any civic value, and by Aristotle's own grounds, perfect friendship must be an achievement of pure goodness, rendering such delimitation contradictory. People who seek out only members of their own racial group are not friends to anyone, most of all themselves.

Aristotle makes equality a condition of perfect friendship, and because he supposed that not all persons are equal, he imagined that it was possible only within a certain class: in an aristocratic society there can be no perfect friendship between an aristocrat and a commoner; even in a democratic society there may be class distinctions that inhibit the cultivation of friendship. But in the nature of things, there is no basis for this sort of inequality, and hewing to a belief in essential inequality is a prejudice.

Even if we cannot be friends with everybody, having friendships cultivates an attitude of friendliness, which is a civic virtue. It involves being a friend to the city, like the virtue of my friend who fixes appliances. According to his method of seeking the mean between extremes, Aristotle locates the virtue of friendliness between being obsequious or servile and being quarrelsome or generally disagreeable. We acquire this virtue through relations with our friends, for being a good friend involves tolerating some faults yet being ready to criticize when it is needed, without ceasing to be a friend. Someone who indiscriminately applauds all that we do is not a friend, but a flatterer. Nor is someone who always finds fault. While Aristotle himself gives no name to this virtue, tradition has designated it "friendliness": a love or affection of one's city and community, a desire to bring about what is truly best for it, and an inclusivity that excludes no one. Friendliness finds expression in a variety of sentiments: neighborliness, sympathy, compassion, a deep yearning for the happiness of all. Friendliness is the tie that binds a city together. It is timeless idea, never more so than now.

Equality and Nature

ARISTOTLE WAS A NATURALIST. He believed that nature comprised the whole of reality, conceiving of nature in two respects: as productive power and as the totality of its products. These products fit together not as a random aggregate of things, but as a well-formed universe ruled by intelligence, and, because that intelligence is self-perpetuating, the results would be eternal.

Now, there are two general kinds of naturalism. One supposes that the productive power of nature has no purpose or end in view, that the products of nature, great and large, are the results of chance, necessity, and mechanical processes. This kind of naturalism is exemplified in Darwin's theory of the origin of species, and by his intellectual ancestors—most notably, Democritus of Abdera whose system of nature was refined by Epicurus and beautifully presented by Lucretius in the Latin poem, *De rerum natura* ("On the nature of things"). Lucretius casts nature as opportunistic rather than purposive, and yet not without fruitful results, some more enduring and more refined than others. That such happy outcomes occur is the good fortune of mice and men.

Aristotle's conception of naturalism differs fundamentally from that of Darwin and his intellectual ancestor Lucretius. Aristotle's system of nature is sometimes characterized as "teleological", meaning that nature always acts purposively, towards some good end, or towards a universe of goods. Nature acts not as a person, but by inherent design. Nature's purpose is always beneficial, towards a functional rather than a dysfunctional end (although Aristotle did admit that natural processes may go awry). When explaining things, he would often make use of a common refrain that nature does nothing in vain. This belief, which from our modern perspective is manifestly false, governed his thoughts about political equality.

He contended that political equality should be granted only to persons who meet certain qualifications. Since nature did not make everyone the same, he concluded that not everyone is fit to be a citizen. To begin with, unlike Plato, Aristotle excluded women; he also excluded those who were not born Greek as well as males who were not well-born on the grounds that they are not educatable and therefore were incapable of becoming virtuous in every respect. He argued that men and women are observably different, that women are generally weaker than men, less bold, and, since nature does nothing in vain, nature must have intended that women should be subject to men, wives to their husbands. In Aristotle's view, patriarchalism should be the rule of the family, and of the city also. Likewise, he observed that some men are strong in body yet weak in mind, and therefore better suited to manual labor than to the more rarified pursuits of the well-born. Such men are by nature fit to be servants or slaves, never citizens, and since nature does nothing in vain, to limit their social prospects to menial roles and subject them to the rule of well-born virtuous masters is just, according to nature. Yet, Aristotle was also forced to admit that the evidence is not conclusive: in *Politics*, he remarks that some of the well-born do not meet the physical standards of gentility, which requires refinement of figure or gracefulness, in contrast to the brute strength of the servile classes. In such instances we must suppose that people's souls, which we cannot see, match their respective social roles, the sort of remark that should only be made with tongue in cheek.

    I must pause to clarify that political equality as we now understand it is not a principle grounded in nature but in equity, which is to say, in fairness and impartiality; it is a principle of practical reason or good sense, a pragmatic idea. What this means is that all persons within a legal jurisdiction have an equal right to fair and impartial treatment under the law, and they are subject to its demands and penalties so long as they are able to understand what the law prescribes. This modern notion of equality has its roots in the naturalism of Darwin and Lucretius, who supposed that every individual is different. To be sure, species evolve, and in some of them certain characteristics dominate more than others. But even here there are differences: even male and female is not an exact difference—variations are many, which is why a person's gender is best judged by what they take it to be. The same applies to the color, form, and size of our bodies, and to the number and shape of our limbs, and the disposition and capabilities of our minds. None of these differences have any moral or political value or application. All fall under the general rule, treat everyone the same, with a feeling of fairness that is attentive to their particular differences and needs. Yet, leaping forward to our American present, we should also remind ourselves that the framers of our constitution (who were slave owners), and "the People of the United States" who established that document as the supreme law of the land were men who did not mean to grant political equality to women or slaves. True equality has come slowly, and has not yet been perfectly realized.

Back to Aristotle: he supposed that only males qualify as citizens, and of these, only the heads of households. A city, or *polis*, is a composite organization of citizens and their households. Within the household, the head of household rules as king; he is a gentleman, who has no other social function but to engage in politics and philosophy and oversee his property. All menial tasks are performed by slaves or servants.

Not surprisingly, Aristotle's preference for inequality carries over into his account of the three main types of government: monarchic, aristocratic, or republican, as well as their attendant corruptions. A king stands apart from his subjects as a father from his children, ruling for their sake while theoretically always acting for their benefit. A corrupt king, a tyrant or despot, rules as a slave-master; his subjects have no rights; their role in life is to serve his interests and gratify his desires.

In contrast, aristocracy is the rule of the most qualified. Aristotle preferred it above all other forms of government, for he believed that every human society divides naturally into two groups: aristocrats and the masses. Hence, he considered it the most natural of regimes. Oligarchy, its evil twin, is the rule of the rich and privileged, dwellers in proud towers in the central city, or in country estates—lovers of luxury, conspicuous consumers, a counterfeit elite.

Last is constitutionalism—Aristotle uses the term Greek terms *politeia*, or *politeuma*, to denote a form of rule based on fundamental law, a sort of republicanism. Curiously, to illustrate this sort of rule, Aristotle cited the rule of a husband over his wife. He regarded marriage—mistakenly—as a partnership, where the woman is the lesser partner, subject to rules, but to rational rules, with valid reasons, and so he was forced to admit that a woman is a rational being, although not equal to her husband in capability and power.

Finally, Aristotle considered democracy, the rule of the people, to be an unstable seedbed of tyranny, for he feared that the people were imprudent, not susceptible to the rule of reason, deluded by populist fantasies and passions. This should be a warning to us. Aristotle was speaking from experience.

The City as a School of Virtue

According to Aristotle, not every settlement of persons is a city. What qualifies a settlement as a city is how effectively it enables its inhabitants to live a good life. To that end, a city must provide for various things: a secure site, urban planning, and sanitation; public tranquility, health, and a just way to settle disputes; defense against foreign enemies, commerce sufficient to guarantee a comfortable life, and education. These conditions promote a common good, but for Aristotle, they are not enough. A city must also be a place whose institutions and laws are designed to make its citizens truly good, living lives that are virtuous and just. And since Aristotle supposed that only the virtuous can be happy, a city must promote happiness as well. One that does this well is just, or in accordance with right reason, because it does everything right.

Consistent with his naturalism, Aristotle expected that a just government would ensure a common good, according to which social goods would be distributed according to each person's natural capacity to use them. The rule of law, of right reason, must be comprehensive and aim at this all-inclusive good. True justice always does good, never harm. In all these respects, Aristotle follows Plato in regarding the city as first and foremost a school of virtue.

Perhaps no idea so clearly differentiates ancients from moderns as this. We moderns tend to regard morality as a private matter, and although everyone would agree that teaching children right from wrong is important, no one would want this to become the chief business of the state. Perhaps this is because, today, widespread corruption has led many to believe that all governments are immoral, their officials motivated by greed and a lust for power. Yet, if that is the condition of our government, we have little reason to believe that individually we are any better. We too often mistake resentment towards the wrongs of others for a moral passion. I am reminded of a book entitled *Moral Man and Immoral Society*, first published in 1932 by the theologian Reinhold Niebuhr, with whom I once studied. In this still-timely book, Niebuhr ridicules the illusion of private morality and proves its public irrelevance; he also has uncomplimentary things to say about moral optimists who fail to recognize the intractable forces of injustice and of greed, in public and private life.

James Madison, a principal framer of the Constitution, was also under no illusions when he wrote: "If men were angels, no government would be necessary. If angels were to govern men, neither external nor internal controls on government would be necessary. In framing a government which is to be administered by men over men, the great difficulty lies in this: you must first enable the government to control the governed; and in the next place oblige it to control itself". As he saw it, a city is not a school of virtue but a sanctuary of law that protects its citizens from oppression and from the insolence of government officials. But even Madison was forced to admit that our system of law relied on citizens choosing more or less virtuous leaders who would infuse the mechanism of government with a moral resolve and purpose, thereby purifying it. He supposed that a fundamental law, properly constituted, would oblige a government to control itself. But self-control is a virtue. So, the rule of law must teach virtue, perhaps not in a formal manner, but indirectly using law to promote a common practice of seeking first the public good.

Like us, Plato and Aristotle lived in times of crisis and were in search of a method to negotiate the rapids of political disorder and to preserve justice. This is why they wrote their books, and why we read them. In an earlier essay, I mentioned that Aristotle wrote the *Politics* when the Greek *polis* was in jeopardy. Alexander, his sometime pupil, had a lust for conquest but also a quaint fondness for Greek cities. Following the conquest of a new country he would found a Greek city as a monument to his achievement. Aristotle may have seen an opportunity in this practice. Clearly, he had a conservative goal: to preserve the idea of the city as a school of virtue. It was a noble purpose. He was not naïve. Rather he understood what he was up against, which comes through in his account of the economy of the city, of what it should be and what it might become when its horizons are global.

Our word "economics" is derived from the Greek term *oikonomike*, which describes the art of household management—something which all heads of household must master, if they are to prosper. In the *Politics*, Aristotle enquires whether this includes the art of getting rich and of dealing in money. One must keep in mind that Aristotle believed that the wealth of a city should reside in its households. The wealth of a household consists of the goods and personnel that are needed to meet the needs of living. Aristotle also acknowledges that wealth is accumulated through commerce, by those who supply the goods and services on which all households depend. Namely, merchants and tradesmen. Money is needed for acquisition of goods and services, so the householder has need of it. The question is how much?

Money and trade are necessary for the household's wellbeing, and therefore for the wellbeing of the city, but only so long as they are employed to provide for natural needs and modest comforts of life. Trading in money, usury, and the building of large trading conglomerates to acquire wealth without limit are unnatural practices to be scorned. In the face of a changing world, Aristotle worried that the acquisition of great wealth, which was going on all about him, would corrupt the city and ruin the land, making it unusable for meeting the ordinary needs of modest households. In short, he grew aware that greed fostered political and environmental degradation, and because greed is a vice that operates without limit, the devastation that it could cause might be total.

This is a familiar concern that unites the ancient and modern world. It should be our concern too. But how do we remedy it? Aristotle's remedy was by causing the city to become a school of virtue; a modern solution, was to make it a sanctuary of law.

The modern solution was Machiavelli's.

MACHIAVELLI

Ancients and Moderns

Nicolò Machiavelli (1469–1527) has been described as the first modern. To begin to understand him and the age in which he lived, one must try to imagine Italy during his lifetime. Historians describe the period as a time of transition, the end of the Renaissance and the beginning of the modern era. It was a period of war and political disorder brought on by the rise of nation-states, their imperial expansion, and by cruel religious conflict. Italy proved a battleground, and its independent cities turned into pawns in a contest between predatory nations surrounding her: France, Spain, The Holy Roman Empire—which would later devolve into the Austro-Hungarian Empire, whose troubles climaxed in the first World War. On top of all of these, there were also the Swiss, who likewise entertained desires to become masters of Italy; and the Popes, militant princes, and priest-kings, who were major players in the struggle for political power in Europe.

Machiavelli was a poet, playwright, citizen, and sometime public official of Florence, who also wrote two works that are now regarded as classics of political philosophy: *The Prince* and *Discourses on Livy*. Scholars describe him as the first modern political thinker. Yet his mind was ancient: rooted in an ancient conjecture that has been refined and amply confirmed through scientific evidence during the last century and a half. In this view, nature is conceived as a limitless power capable of generating worlds upon worlds throughout a constantly expanding space-time. There is no meaning to this process; it is, for all we know, without beginning or end or purpose, a ceaseless process producing worlds, galaxies, and lesser cosmic systems in an endless sequence. Our planet, our solar system, our galaxy, and universe are mere moments in a never-ending sequence. Our existence is here and now, and if it is to have any meaning or purpose, we must provide it.

      This idea has its roots in early Greek philosophy, before Plato and Aristotle. These early Greek philosophers developed curiosity about the nature of things; indeed, in the course of their inquiries, chemical and astronomical, and through their tentative explanations, they invented the modern idea of nature. The most complete account of their thoughts was written up by the Roman poet Lucretius in his great epic poem, *De rerum natura*, a poem that was forgotten and virtually lost; in 1416, Poggio Bracciollini, also a Florentine and Renaissance scholar, discovered a manuscript of Lucretius' poem in a German monastery. It was copied and widely disseminated; Machiavelli made a copy for his own use, added his own comments in the margins. That copy now resides in the Vatican Library.

Lucretius' poem contained the seeds of modern thought, not only in physics and cosmology, but in law and the theory of government. By this account, there is no eternal law and no ideal form of government. Law and the institutions of government are conventional things, schemes of order and fairness imagined, proposed, and mutually accepted as suitable means of establishing peace and stability in an otherwise troubled social world. They are experiments in living.

It is against this intellectual background that we can begin to understand what Machiavelli has written, and while not all that we read may please us, all of it is instructive; his writings are a mirror of humanity, of the world, and of how and how not to live in it together.

Postscript:

Someone reading this essay may think that in writing about ancients and moderns, I have ignored what came between: The Middle Ages. Indeed, if I were writing a comprehensive history of political thought, this would be a serious, unforgivable omission. The gap has been filled by the work of R.W. and A.J. Carlyle's *A History of Medieval Political Theory in the West*, a lovely, expansive work, learned, clear, concise, and available online.

Machiavelli's *The Prince*

If I were asked to recommend required reading in the education of every citizen, I would choose the political works of Machiavelli, namely *The Prince* and *Discourses on Livy*. The sober realism of both works is reason enough for my choice, but others will emerge.

The two works may seem on the face of it very different, because they treat contrary themes. *The Prince* is about principalities, or the rule of one individual whose power is unrivaled and for whom law is a mere instrument of control; the theme of *Discourses on Livy* is republicanism, the rule of many under the rule of law. Yet, if you read them together, their contents often overlap, and it becomes clear that *The Prince* is a spin-off from the much longer *Discourses*.

Machiavelli does not champion one form of government over the other. Rather he analyzes them, and the circumstances where one works and the other may not, basing his judgments on both historical precedent and present circumstances. In this respect, the two works are very similar in method and manner. Machiavelli wrote them during the same period of his life. He had served for almost a decade and a half as a high official in the Florentine republic, a role which came to an end in 1512, when the Medici overthrew the republic and ruled the city as autocrats. Machiavelli was removed from office, imprisoned, tortured, and finally released, whereupon he retired to his farm not far from the city.

But he greatly desired to return to an active public life, he needed employment; the Medici may have caused his downfall, but they were princes and had the power to restore his fortune. Hence, he wrote *The Prince*, and dedicated it to Lorenzo de Medici—not the famous Lorenzo the Magnificent, but his grandson and namesake, who then ruled Florence, with support from his uncle Pope Leo X. Machiavelli's tone in *The Prince* is sober and, even clinical, until the final chapter, where he expresses the urgent hope that a princely figure will raise an army from the people and free Italy from her foreign oppressors.

What prompted him to write *The Prince* may be explained by a remark written in a chapter of the *Discourses* (Bk. I, Ch. 17): Machiavelli writes that when a people have become corrupt, when through selfishness, resentment, and indifference to law, the citizens of a republic lose the ability to act as citizens and to govern themselves, their political health and freedom can be restored only by a power independent of themselves—that is, by a prince, who "with enormous power" restores the rule of law and revives the customs and way of life that undergird them. He did not believe that republican rule was likely to be restored in Florence, his native city, in any other way, and he was pessimistic even about that.

But *The Prince* is not a manifesto; in his writings, Machiavelli always remains cool and analytic. In a letter to a friend, he confesses that politics or political commentary fills his mind every day, all day long, and that he can think or talk about nothing else. It was not mere curiosity but an existential anguish that prompted him. His letters are ample proof of this; they are filled with political analyses and draft policies. Machiavelli writes passionately, to be sure, but, as one biographer put it, his writing displays a controlled passion that steeled his intellect and gave a knife-edge to his thoughts, enabling him to cut ever deeper into political reality past and present. If one must live in time, Machiavelli believed, then one must become its master.

So how should a prince rule? In a princely manner, of course. But what is that? It involves virtue and facing up to fortune. However, by "virtue", Machiavelli means something different from what Plato or Aristotle meant; he means a capability to prevail over all the machinations of one's rivals and to withstand the setbacks of fate or fortune—indeed, to exploit them. A prince's virtue consists of the cunning of a fox and the ferocity of a lion, of cool reason and a readiness to act boldly. It includes also an iron will and exquisite self-control. These are the virtues of Machiavelli's prince. Moral goodness is not his goal. Rather it is the survival of his princedom:

> The divide that separates how one lives
> and how one ought to live is such that
> anyone who abandons what needs to be

> done in favor of what ought to be done achieves his downfall rather than his preservation. A man who wishes to profess [moral] goodness at all times will come to ruin among so many who are not good. Therefore, it is necessary for a prince who wishes to maintain himself to learn how not to be good, and to use this knowledge or not to use it according to necessity.

Much depends upon how one discerns political necessity. It is not a matter of having clear values on which to base one's judgments of what is to be done: political judgment derives from clearly discerning one's situation, from a knowledge of past successes and failures, and from one's own experience. Nor is it true that Machiavelli was advocating gross immorality. He was a realist, who perceived the inherent conflicts and moral ambiguity in political action, and not a proponent of political wickedness or of egomania.

One last point. I remarked earlier that what may have motivated Machiavelli to write *The Prince* was his desire to find a solution to the political disorder in his city and nation, which made them easy prey to other powers. His fear that a people may have become so corrupt that they would be unable to prevail politically led him to think it necessary to create another power, an autocracy, independent of the people, who would be their savior. This same problem was addressed by James Madison in *The Federalist no. 51*. Madison was well aware of Machiavelli's solution to the problem and he rejected it. The idea of looking to a prince as a savior of the people was too dangerous to be considered. He proposed rather to hold fast to the rule of law, and to a fundamental law that prohibits the concentration of power in one person or agency.

This is the central idea of modern republicanism. Machiavelli too recognized that a self-styled autocrat, posing as a constitutional executive, is more likely to corrupt a people than save them and may well lead them to a state that is beyond redemption. In these dangerous times, we must be wary of princes or demagogues bearing gifts, and also mindful of corruption in our midst.

Living in Dark Times with Livy

THE TITLE OF MACHIAVELLI'S BOOK, *Discourses on Livy*, requires an explanation. Livy (Titus Livius; 59 BCE–17 CE) was a Roman historian, a contemporary of Caesar Augustus, who wrote a history of Rome from its founding until his own day (*De urbi condita libri*—"*Books from the founding of the city*"). He witnessed the decline of the Roman Republic and the establishment of the Roman imperial Principate by Caesar Augustus, a transition that he describes as "the dark dawning of our modern day, when we can neither endure our vices nor face the remedies needed to cure them". His work is an elegy, perhaps a *cri de Coeur*, for a passing excellence:

> I hope my passion for Rome's past has not impaired my judgment for I do honestly believe that no country has ever been greater or purer than ours or richer in good citizens and noble deeds; none has been free for so many generations from the vices or avarice and luxury; nowhere have thrift and plain-living been for so long held in such esteem. Indeed, poverty, with us, went hand in hand with contentment. Of late years, wealth has made us greedy, and self-indulgence has brought us, through every form of sensual excess, to be, if I may so put it, in love with death both individual and collective.

Readers of this essay may wonder, "Why bother about Rome and Roman historians?". I would respond first by calling attention to the remarkable durability of ancient Rome, a durability made possible by its laws and political institutions. The city was founded in the middle of the 8th century BCE, and for two and one-half centuries it was ruled by a succession of kings. In 509 BCE a revolution occurred, wherein the monarchy was abolished and replaced by a republic that continued for nearly five centuries; during this period Rome established an empire that, according to the historian Polybius (200–118 BCE), ranged over almost "the whole of the inhabited world"—an overstatement, to be sure, but the vastness of the empire is nonetheless remarkable. Even after the end of republican rule, the laws and institutions founded during the Republic enabled the empire to last for almost another 500 years notwithstanding its many dysfunctions. There are lessons to be learned here, and Livy is a good teacher.

Since the decline of Rome, empires have come and gone: the Spanish, French, German, and Russian. The British Empire, which some of us still remember, and to which we once belonged, could claim a vaster dominion—an "empire on which the sun never set". (Although the Spanish beat them to it, though theirs lasted a mere three and a half centuries, if that long). The American Republic, our so-called "Empire of Liberty", is barely two and a half centuries old and now seems to be in trouble. The same abuses that Livy supposed to signal the Roman Republic's downfall prevail today: excessive greed, selfishness, vain ambition, political dysfunction, rival factions, and the abuse of executive power. We, too, are living in dark times, which, of course, is not to suppose that our past is full of light and innocence.

Times like these should make us reflective and turn our attention to history, if for no other reason than to find consolation where all hopes fail. We learn from Livy how many of our basic institutions have Roman precedents, and at the very least, like Livy, we may take pride in them because of their excellence. The greatest of these is the rule of an impartial law as a guarantee of liberty. The opening sentence of Livy's second book epitomizes this point of view: "My task from now on will be to trace the history of a free nation, governed by annually elected officers of state and subject not to the caprice of individual men, but to the overriding authority of law".

Looking back, Livy writes of the founding of a republic, which as I have said, lasted almost five hundred years. In the new Roman constitution, the monarchy was replaced by two chief executives, or Consuls, who were elected annually from the Senate; they also served as commanders-in-chief of the Roman armies; upon their election, they drew lots to decide which of them should carry the emblem of head of state, but in all other respects they had equal if not rival power. (Perhaps the framers of our constitution also should have considered a dual presidency). Within the Republic, the Senate continued as an aristocratic body, but the people were now also empowered by law; they had their own representatives, the Tribunes of the People, elected from their own ranks, who had authority to veto any legislation that they believed violated the rights and interests of those they represented. As well, the Tribunes were authorized to summon a people's assembly, which had legislative power. Thus was created, if not the first, then certainly the most accomplished political system of checks and balances in the ancient world. Conflict and rivalry did not end, but their excesses were regulated and channeled by law. Livy's history describes how all this came to be, how it happened, and the passion and heartache that accompanied it.

The hero of the founding of the Roman Republic was Lucius Junius Brutus (not to be confused with Marcus Junius Brutus, the assassin of Caesar, who also was a heroic defender of the Republic). This "first Brutus" led the revolt that overthrew the last Roman king, Lucius Tarquinius Superbus, and ended the monarchy. Brutus had two sons, young and impressionable, who were persuaded to join a conspiracy to restore the monarchy. They were apprehended, and because their father had been elected consul in the new government, it was his duty to condemn them and witness their execution. "Throughout the pitiful scene [their public execution] all eyes were on the father's face, where a father's anguish was plain to see". This truly was to follow the letter of the law.

Postscript:

Livy's *History* contained 142 books, of which only 35 have survived. These have been translated and are available in English in paperback editions, published by Penguin and Oxford World Classics. Consult your local bookseller. Also worth reading are Edward Gibbon's classic, *The History of the Decline and Fall of the Roman Empire*, and for a short readable history of Rome, Mary Beard's *SPQR, A History of Ancient Rome* [*SPQR* is an acronym signifying the official name of the Roman state*: Senatus PopulusQue Romanus*—"The Senate and People of Rome"].

Machiavelli's *Discourses on Livy*

WITHOUT DOUBT, Machiavelli's *Discourses on Livy* is unsurpassed among works of political philosophy. Neither Plato's *Republic*, nor the Laws, nor Aristotle's *Ethics* and *Politics* stand above it. It is far more readable too, a browser's delight, and easy to navigate. Machiavelli began writing the *Discourses* soon after his forced retirement, around 1512, but unlike *The Prince*, he lingered over it, and the book remained a work-in-progress until he died 1527. Writing it gave him consolation.

Unlike his illustrious predecessors and successors, Machiavelli does not start off with a declaration of fundamental principles derived from mere reason, but with examples from history. I do not mean that Machiavelli was unprincipled—as is commonly supposed. He employed an inductive method, deriving principles from well-tried practices, which is why he chose Livy's work of history as his primary source. *Discourses* reads like a user's manual. Each chapter, regardless of length, treats a substantial topic. The shortest (I. 42), at less than a page, observes how easily men are corrupted, even those who are well-educated and otherwise well-reputed, and why it is necessary to have laws to restrain them from evil-doing. The longest chapter (III. 6) is about conspiracies; it discusses the motives that lead to them, the hazards of engaging in them, and how best to defeat them. It should be required reading for all conspiracy theorists—they may be enlightened by it—and anyone else with an interest in current politics.

Nowhere in the book does Machiavelli bother with ideals or ideal narratives. He writes about the past, recent or remote, describing the actions of princes and peoples along with their outcomes. He never fails to be enlightening, even though he is also troubling. For example, in Bk. II, Ch. 8, all about wars of conquest, he compares the conquests of princes or imperial republics, like Rome before the Caesars, with those of migrating peoples. The former enlarge their empires by subjecting other nations to their rule; their purpose is mere acquisition, and so they are willing to allow their newly conquered subjects to retain their ancestral land and to continue to live according to their own laws and customs so long as they remain peaceful. However, when entire peoples and their families are driven by famine, or war, or oppression, or imagine themselves led by God to seek another land, their desire is not just to rule over it, "but, rather, to possess it, even private property, and to drive out or murder its ancient inhabitants". Machiavelli adds the comment: "This kind of war is extremely cruel and frightful", which he intended as a statement of fact and not as a moral judgment. It is calculated nonetheless to open the minds of his readers to political reality and its inherent cruelty. His explanation should enlighten and disturb us, because it fits too well events in the founding of our own nation and its western expansion and the motives of the early settlers to possess the land as though it were an unsettled wilderness, which it was not.

Related to this is the two-faced policy Roman conquerors employed to increase Rome's population—for without a growing populace, a city cannot become great. The policy relied on the joint use of love and force, "by keeping the pathways open and safe" for immigrants, while at the same time destroying nearby cities and enslaving their inhabitants (II. 3). The policy of love is the seed of the beautiful idea of a nation of immigrants. But we have not outgrown the policy of force.

There are many more illuminating and disturbing moments in Machiavelli's book, but there is room here for only one more. I have selected the first chapter of the third book (III. 1), because, more than any other, it offers a key to understanding the whole work. Machiavelli imagines that a civil society functions like a living body; though mortal, it can live long and prosper if it does two things. The first may be likened to setting up exercises: those states live longest that renew themselves by constantly returning to their beginnings.

Machiavelli explains that this is so because the good that a republic is supposed to embody, and which is the source of its health, is most abundantly present in its beginning or founding. The preamble of our constitution may serve as an example of such good, since it tells us why the People of the United States have established the constitution: "to form a more perfect union, establish justice, ensure domestic tranquility, provide for the common defense, promote the general welfare, and secure the blessings of liberty, to ourselves and our posterity". This is all the good that a civil society needs to live a long and happy life, to continue as a whole nation of integral and well-functioning parts, a just society. It outlines our highest good. When Machiavelli mentioned "the good" in this chapter, he was alluding to Aristotle's notion that political science was the science of the highest human good. And so it is.

The second way that a civil society is able to live a long life is by recognizing the noble achievements of its great personages. He had in mind individuals who occupied high office in the government of Rome, and who remained faithful to the laws, especially those "instituted against men's ruthless ambition and insolence". In this way, he perceived that the laws and institutions of government come alive "through the virtue of single citizens" who exemplified them in action, who bravely endeavored to enforce them and prevailed. This is the sort of leadership that makes institutions noble. Thus, it would seem that Machiavelli was not lacking in principles, in spite of his realism and the ambiguities of political life that he described. Rather he was an advocate of the classical ideal of the noble and the good. He discovered that ideal arising spontaneously in the active life of a political society, in the city. May it long endure!

One last word: Machiavelli, like the ancients, regarded the city, or *polis*, as the archetype of civil society and the highest good. He regarded the city more as a sanctuary of law than a school of virtue, but he nevertheless endeavored to endow it with his own variety of pragmatic virtue. He is our link to ancient values and the first real modern.

HOBBES

Thomas Hobbes, our Contemporary

THE LONG LIFE OF THOMAS HOBBES (1588–1679) encompassed England's greatest crisis and perhaps its darkest hour. That he survived them and even flourished is proof of his ingenuity and adaptability; that he also wrote about them is our very good fortune, for in his writings we encounter the voice of experience unmoved by self-pity or sentimental fantasies, a courageous voice. It is one we very much need to hear today.

England's great crisis lasted twenty years, from 1640 until 1660, during which time, the nation suffered a cruel civil war, regicide, a military coup, and much misery. Hobbes was a close observer of these events, and wrote a book about them, which he entitled *Behemoth*. The behemoth is a great beast described in the book of Job (40: 15–24), a monstrous creature, like a massive elephant, capable with his great trunk of drinking up an entire river. He is a symbol of the power of wild Nature or of God, which for Hobbes were the same thing. It is Hobbes' way of representing the terrible power let loose in the land, or the power of God in the hands of men, a power that, once released, they could not control, and which would bring about their ruin.

Hobbes was born in 1588, which was the year of the Great Armada, the large naval fleet that Philip II of Spain, consumed by religious zeal and imperial ambitions, had assembled in preparation for the invasion of England. In an autobiography, Hobbes writes that at the time of his birth, rumors of imminent invasion were abroad in the land, and under such stress "my Mother dear did bring forth Twins at once, both Me and Fear". Fear became his constant companion; one could employ another analogy and say that Hobbes, who never married, wedded himself to it. Yet Hobbes' fear was not pathological. He was too much a realist to give way to subjective moods. The object of his fear was power, especially as wielded by ambitious monarchs, under the sway of their scheming ministers; by revolutionaries, or religious fanatics, or both together occupying one brain; by unscrupulous financiers and the very rich; and by all who in so many various ways attempt to exercise dominion over others, some with the sword, others by offering bribes, or by words from the mouths of ambitious orators who make false promises. It was Hobbes, among all the early modern political thinkers who first caught sight of this monstrous power, and wisely advised that we must fear it and, under the prod of this fear, learn to make peace through the instrument of civil government, for only then can we hope to find safety in this world.

The English Civil War began as a conflict between King and Parliament, which might have been resolved had it not grown entangled in another deeper and more bitter conflict concerning religion. Although England had been declared Protestant by Henry VIII, it was not until the reign of Elizabeth I that its transition from a Catholic to a Protestant nation was completed, the Church of England molded into an established institution of government and religion. Religious zeal was pacified—for a time. However, the Elizabethan Religious Settlement was not well-received by many of her more radical Protestant subjects, some of whom regarded it as a shameful compromise that put politics above religion. The Church of England retained the hierarchy of bishops and archbishops, a hierarchy with which radical Protestants took exception. And it made a secular monarch—in this case, a woman, Elizabeth the First—head of the church.

Protestant pulpits became platforms of protest, and their occupants were more often than not preachers of sedition. First, it was English Presbyterians, who demanded the abolition of the office of bishop and the rule of the church by counsels of clergy. Their adherents gained supremacy in Parliament, which began proceedings against the King, Charles I, for failure to acknowledge their authority. They demanded that civil government conform to their system of ecclesiastical government. Moreover, they declared themselves commanders-in-chief of the militia, forbidding the King to raise an army without their approval.

The conflict grew more acute; more radical religious voices were heard—specifically, Independents, who recognized no religious authority but the Bible and the free interpretation of it, and considered any monarch an abomination. They claimed liberty in all matters religious and demanded toleration for themselves, although not for other religious sorts, and none for any who practiced no religion or acknowledged no god. Cautious Presbyterians feared that these Independents had gone too far, and some of them began to wonder whether they should not shift their support to the King. In the end, the more radical faction of the Independents won out: they accused the King of making war on his people and declared an end to the monarchy. The King was made a prisoner, tried, and, in 1649, beheaded. England was then declared a commonwealth. The Independents found their champion in Thomas Cromwell, a skilled military tactician, relentless self-promoter, religious fanatic, and political realist.

A third feature of the English revolution was the ongoing colonial and industrial expansion, which enabled the creation of great estates, the amassing of great fortunes, as well as the exploitation of the working classes, the recourse to slavery for additional labor, and the spread of political corruption. There was a fourth feature, too: the failure of universities, institutions of higher learning, to honor truth; as though truth were something that one invents rather than discovers. It seems in that age, as perhaps in ours, political leaders, university professors, and the public had lost the capacity to deal in truth and preferred to dwell in their own fantasies.

Hobbes is our contemporary because all the forces that were unleashed during his time are abroad today, although wearing different masks. Presbyterians and Independents (ancestors of Congregationalists) have turned benign and politically irrelevant. But the powers of discord and political madness are at large, their effects present in ethnic hatred, in the narcissistic culture of the super-rich, and in demagoguery. In the absence of reason, our public discourse has turned into a seedbed for political opportunists. We have much to fear.

Hobbes' Politics

An outstanding feature of Thomas Hobbes' political theory is its clarity and simplicity. It is founded on two simple principles: natural right and natural law. Natural right, or the right of nature, is the liberty or freedom of persons to act in whatever way they choose; natural law consists of the duties that every person is obligated by nature to do. Rights and duties are conflicting warrants: If I have a natural right to do something, there can be no valid law of nature prohibiting it; if a law of nature prohibits me from an action, then I cannot claim a right to do it.

Hobbes affirmed there is one primary or fundamental right of nature attributable not only to every human being, but also to every living creature capable of voluntary action. This is a right to self-defense or, more generally, to self-preservation, "the preservation of one's own nature". This includes the use of whatever means may be available to enact it; the right extends beyond the mere right to exist to encompass the will to be free and self-determining. No law, natural or civil, can negate it or abridge this absolute and inalienable right. Hobbes remarked that even condemned criminals have the right to escape from their captors, which is why they are led bound and under guard to their execution.

There is no doubt that, by introducing this notion, Hobbes unleashed a powerful idea into the world. Because of it, any law that in any way puts the life or limb of an individual or groups of persons under the arbitrary control or jurisdiction of another is deprived of all legitimacy. Hobbes' definition of natural right makes slavery impermissible, and it also negates the presumed right of husbands to be lords over their wives. A woman's right to an abortion is grounded in this natural right; so, also, the right of individuals to decide on their gender identity, whom to marry, and, paradoxically, when to die. Hobbes did not foresee all of the consequences that would flow from this principle, but I am inclined to believe that if he had the gift of foreknowledge, he would not have been shocked or disappointed.

Now, Hobbes observed that a state of nature, if there ever was one, would be a state of war of all against all, for there would be no civil government to protect or prevent one individual from killing another, which everyone would have the right to do to insure their own self-preservation. Where there is no government or judicial authority, who is to decide but oneself on the need to kill another for one's own protection, or how best to gain retribution for any harm that another may have caused us? Anger, fear, and paranoia are the final arbiters in a state of nature. There is no way that individuals can make themselves immune to this dangerous condition or be secure from it, for it should be evident that even the strongest man can be killed by the weakest man. Or, as Hobbes noted, by a woman. This, by the way, was, for Hobbes, proof of complete human equality—not just among men, but inclusive of women. He understood that the rights of women are equal to those of men in every respect. He was after all born during the reign of Elizabeth the Great.

Because war is a constant danger and threat to one's being, it evokes chronic fear and misery. This unhappy state of mankind—constant danger and the fear of it—must remain everyone's companion, until war and the very threat of it ceases. Nevertheless, Hobbes believed that human beings are rational creatures, and a major part of rational behavior is prudential: considering one's options and choosing to act in a way that will bring about the most beneficial results to oneself. In a chronic state of war, peace must seem the most beneficial and therefore most desirable option of all, for there can be no winners in an endless war. Reflecting on this dire situation, Hobbes conceived his first fundamental law of nature, "Seek peace, and follow it". He supposed that this fundamental law does not in any way contradict the right of nature, which every human being possesses. Rather, it is the perfect complement of the right of nature, for if this law were duly observed by everyone everywhere, there would be no more war, and everyone would be secure from violent death, although we would remain mortal beings.

But how can this be achieved? Here Hobbes' great clarity of intellect is matched by his fertile imagination: he imagined that it is brought about by an act of creation comparable to the divine creation of the world. God created the world, but we humans have created *Leviathan*, which is the title of his great book on political theory. Leviathan is a great sea monster, described in the book of Job, chapter 41; an animal of insuperable strength and ferocity: "He esteemeth iron as straw, and brass as rotten wood; Darts are counted as stubble, he laugheth at the shaking of a spear; Upon earth there is not his like, who is made without fear; He is a king over all the children of pride". Such is a human commonwealth, or civil state, a corporate person in whom we, children of pride, are incorporated as citizens and members of one body politic, Leviathan, and in whom we live, move, and have our being.

But although the creation of civil society is, like the supposed creation of the world, a creation out of nothing, it is not miraculous. The act of creating a civil society is a voluntary act of persons, who covenant with each other, pledging their lives, their fortunes, and their sacred honor, no longer to live apart, but mutually to forego a portion of their natural liberty, specifically their right to use whatever means at hand to protect their lives. They transfer this natural right to another, who now has the power of retribution and punishment, and who in turn pledges to protect and defend *all* the people, to ensure their safety and welfare. Here is where the law of nature truly becomes a law, for in this new great society, all citizens oblige themselves to obedience to its laws and fidelity to its institutions without limit of duration. They also put themselves under a new fear, the fear of Leviathan, who will punish them if they fail to keep their promises—for a promise once made may be broken, but the obligation to keep it never ceases, nor does the threat of retribution.

I believe that Hobbes was truly awed by this thing which we call the civil state, and it is truly an amazing thing, notwithstanding the dreary history of corruption in governments, of civil wars, betrayals, and revolutions. What is most awesome of all is the burden that it places on all of us who by virtue of being citizens are participants in the promise to seek peace and follow it.

Postscript:

It should be noted that unlike other political philosophers, Hobbes did not suppose that civil societies had any higher purpose than the peace and welfare of its citizens. He was not obsessed by visions of greatness, of manifest destiny, cultural pride, imperial expansion, or human exceptionalism. His only concern was for peace

Lingering Problems with Hobbes

THERE ARE PROBLEMS WITH HOBBES' political theory. To begin with, the political solution that I described in the previous essay is a prescription against anarchy, but the remedy prescribed is extreme: a strong dose of absolutism. It seems that in his scheme of civil government, Hobbes has given all power to the sovereign and none to the people; the sovereign's right is to command, the people's duty is to hear and obey. According to his hypothetical account of the origin of civil government, the people are the creators of it—they enter into it, submitting to its power and jurisdiction by an irrevocable promise, which is their free act and deed. Their reasons for submitting to this "mortal God" (Hobbes ironic name for the civil state) is to escape from a chronic state of war, where peace or war are the only two options. Yet, it seems that in choosing peace, the people behave like an anxious flock of chickens who, fearing the unavoidable danger of the free range, build a henhouse for themselves and agree to make a fox their keeper.

Moreover, when Hobbes wrote about the origin of the civil state, he did not have in mind a particular moment in human history when wandering bands of human beings abandoned their uncertain nomadic existence and agreed to gather into societies, establish permanent settlements, and submit to a common rule. He was aware that what he wrote about the origin of the civil state was mere hypothesis, a plausible fiction.

On top of all this there is Hobbes' low regard for human nature. He believed that all human beings are selfish and afraid, lacking any inherent nobility, and, besides, we are not free. But if all this were true, if we were indeed so petty and self-seeking, and incapable to act except as passion drives us, how did Hobbes suppose we could ever transform ourselves into citizens who are committed to equality and the rule of law, and even more into brave and fair-minded political leaders, whose only concern is to protect their subjects and promote the general welfare?

These problems are not reasons to turn away from Hobbes, but to look deeper. Hobbes' depths are not murky and mystical: they consist of clear, transparent, albeit rigorous thoughts. He approached politics as an experimental naturalist, his plausible fiction about how civil societies develop a hypothesis. All scientific hypotheses originate in this way, inventions of reason designed to make sense out of the regularities that occur in nature. Keen observers of these regularities imagine how the forces producing them may be directed towards other ends and they devise experiments to test and refine their imagined hypothesis. This is the process of experimental science. Hobbes was a political scientist who employed an empirical method, fashioning his political hypothesis by studying history, which was a source of examples and confirmations. He never supposed there was a single moment in human history where mankind created civil society. History taught him that the process happened repeatedly and that there were as many, if not more, failures as successes.

Hobbes regarded political science as a practical science, like medicine or engineering. Civil societies do not evolve; they must be made, and there are better or worse ways of making them. Thus, politics is an art grounded in knowledge of human nature. To use such knowledge well, one must be unsentimental and realistic. Hobbes was acutely aware of the anarchic tendencies in human societies, the predatory methods of political opportunists and ambitious demagogues, who promised peace and prosperity but delivered only conflict and inequality. So he prescribed strong measures to overcome them. His low opinion of the human character was repeatedly confirmed by the events of his day.

But despite his pessimism, Hobbes, more than any other modern political thinker clearly saw the enormity of the task that faces every generation of humanity. Or, perhaps, his vision was clarified by virtue of his pessimism, for he was under no illusions. He realized that if we are to live together in peace, then we must become citizens, and we become citizens only by transforming ourselves into something higher and nobler than selfish creatures. He believed that this was possible because human beings, albeit corrupt or corruptible, selfish and self-aggrandizing, are also capable of using reason to fashion laws whose validity is self-evident to all. "Seek peace, and follow it" requires no justification. And from this basic law of nature, others may be derived. Prominent among them, the following: that promises once made must be kept; that fair value be agreed upon for goods and services; that these goods and services be equitably distributed; and that extreme poverty and extreme wealth are social evils. Furthermore, sentiments of gratitude and good will are essential to peaceful social relations; we ought not to seek revenge, but be ready to pardon others who offend us; and we must forswear all attitudes of contempt for others and all acts of cruelty. In sum, we must do to others as we would have others do to us, and the converse, that we not do to others what we would not have done to ourselves. By these means, we develop into sociable and mutually accommodating citizens, and if we fail to accomplish this well enough, we fear the fox who stands ready to enforce the law.

But who controls the fox? Hobbes believed that rulers are above the law, not because they are superior beings, but because it goes with the role of a monarch, who, even if bound by an oath, could act as he or she pleased. For there is no one above the ruler with right and power of restraint. Laws alone are not sufficient, for to supreme rulers they are mere marks on a page, mere dictation. And in any case, since all the powers of government—executive, legislative, and judicial—resided in them, monarchs were subject to no law that they could not revise as they pleased. Hobbes did not recognize the principle of the separation of powers.

Hence, monarchs must be self-regulated, which is to say, they must be virtuous. But the only means of accomplishing this is through persuasion and education. In this respect, Hobbes' *Leviathan* falls into a class of works of advice to monarchs, and while any monarch in his day would have been well-advised to read and take it to heart, there was no means beyond sweet reason to ensure that this would happen. Hobbes had firsthand experience of the process of educating kings, having served as tutor to the Prince of Wales, who would become King Charles II, reputed to be an immoralist but no tyrant. So perhaps Hobbes taught him well.

We learn from Hobbes that our political existence is precarious, and that our institutions rest on unsteady foundations. Yet, if we focus on essentials—how to live in peace, what sorts of law are needed, and how to enforce them fairly and equitably while never giving way to complacency that our work has ended—we may enjoy a measure of success. This is the advice of a realist. Times have changed, but not that much; what Hobbes has written still rings true.

Hobbes on Religion

IN HIS DAY, HOBBES WAS SUSPECTED OF ATHEISM. There is no historical evidence supporting this suspicion, neither in his writings, nor in any other surviving historical records about him. Nonetheless, the suspicion is a historical fact. His detractors, who were many, called him "the Monster of Malmesbury", and held him in contempt, because they believed the suspicion true.

It is instructive to consider their reasons. Keep in mind that the label "atheist" was applied loosely in those times, which is not surprising, because it was used as much as a political label as a religious one. It was an odious label, the kind on which political discourse, then as now, seems to thrive. Strictly speaking, an atheist is someone who believes that there is no God or gods, or, even if there is one, they have no regard for mankind. Atheists maintain that God did not create the world, does not exercise providential governance over it, and has not the least interest in the welfare of mankind. These, it may be recalled, were the opinions of Lucretius. Hobbes wrote nothing promoting such beliefs; indeed, he condemned them. Moreover, he described the ideal civil state as a kingdom of God—not the eternal kingdom promised by Christ to an elect body of Christians, which is not of this world, but an earthly realm of limited duration. I will say more about this shortly.

Hobbes was suspected of atheism because he professed materialism, or corporealism. The physical universe, Hobbes claimed, is the aggregate of all bodies, and nothing else; the study of nature is based on the observation of the relative motion and impact of bodies and their effects, a strictly empirical method. The 17th century marked the beginning of the scientific revolution in Europe, and all its advocates, among them Robert Boyle and Isaac Newton, held similar opinions. But Hobbes carried them much further and applied them more rigorously and consistently. He denied the existence of spiritual or immaterial bodies. To him, the very idea of a spiritual body is a contradiction, for bodies are tangible objects that occupy space. He also believed that the human soul is material, and mortal. He regarded even thoughts as physical things, and thinking itself a computational process in which the mind works like a machine. These and other material beliefs made him odious to others. He commented that the very word "spirit" is derived from the Latin "spiritus" which means breath or wind, which are quantifiable aggregates and hence corporeal. He argued from the Bible that angels or messengers from God are also corporeal, for they appear in various guises, their figures visible, their voices audible, their touch tangible.

Moreover, he maintained that the notion of an immaterial spirit is unbiblical, a relic of Greek philosophy.

Hobbes supposed it originated with Plato, and that the many Gods of Greek and Roman mythology were mere idols of the mind, fantasies posing as mysterious bodies only to the credulous, of which there were many then as now. Likewise, popular beliefs in fairies, sprites, demons, and various and sundry spirits of the air—not to mention all other things that bring enchantment to the world, like magic, alchemy, and the occult—are mere projections of an overworked brain, or of a mind untutored by truth. The truths of nature emerge only after a long and sober process of inquiry, discovery, hypothesis, and experiment.

What about the Holy Spirit? Hobbes observed that it is reported in the Gospels when Jesus was baptized by John the Baptist, that the spirit of God descended on him like a dove, and a voice was heard from heaven; it was the voice of God declaring Jesus to be his only son; and thereupon Jesus was led by the Holy Spirit into the wilderness. Hobbes' explanation of what happened is consistent with Trinitarian orthodoxy: the Holy Spirit is the power of God, and Jesus and the Spirit are distinct persons, although of the same substance. That is, both are God, along with God the Father, yet they are God incarnate. Likewise, in the book of Genesis, when God created the world, it is written that the spirit of God moved across the face of the primal chaos. That spirit, wrote Hobbes, was the creative power of God. Likewise, when Christians are baptized, they are supposed to receive the Holy Spirit, which is to say, the power or grace to live a Christian life—analogous, perhaps, to Hobbes' notion of remaking oneself to become a citizen. All of this suggests that Hobbes acknowledged the prevailing English conception of God at the time, the Holy Trinity.

Did Hobbes suppose that God was corporeal? No, he did not. He confessed that he had no idea of what God was like. The divine nature is incomprehensible to us, and beyond that, there is nothing more to say. How, then, could he be sure that there was a God? Hobbes invoked a standard philosophical argument, based on the common assumption that nothing happens without a cause, and therefore, the universe itself must have a cause, for he assumed that nature is neither eternal nor self-originating. This brings us back to his notion of the Kingdom of God.

Remember Hobbes' claim that a civil state originates when a group of persons covenant with each other to create a civil society, over which they place a sovereign power, a monarch or a supreme assembly, possessing supreme power legislative and judicial power. Yet Hobbes believed that to be a citizen in such a civil state involves more than mere obedience. We are rational beings and should have the capacity to discover a universal law of nature—for if a state of universal and lasting peace is ever to be achieved, all persons everywhere must agree on a common law, a law of nature, a law enacted and enforced not only by monarchs but by the supreme power of the universe, namely God. This Hobbes calls "the right of nature, whereby God reigneth over men, and who punisheth those that break his laws", deriving it not from the fact that God is the first cause or creator of the world (as though he needed our gratitude for this), "but from his irresistible power". Conscious awareness of God's omnipotence, or irresistible power, is supposed keep us all in line, citizens and monarchs. In the light of this line of thinking, Hobbes concluded that the only stable civil society is a theocracy, a Kingdom of God in nature.

So why would anyone suppose that Hobbes was an atheist? Scholars who continue to maintain this opinion acknowledge that Hobbes professed theism, yet they are sure that he didn't mean what he said: his professions of theism were ironic, designed to convey just the opposite of what he appeared to profess. They imagine him to be a very clever atheist. Atheist or not, he was surely clever.

Postscript:

For anyone interested in Hobbes' reputed duplicity, and for a strong case against it, there are two recent works worth reading: *Taming the Leviathan* by Jon Parkin, and *The Two Gods of Leviathan* by A.P. Martinich. They are scholarly works, but very readable. Consult your local bookstore.

SPINOZA

Spinoza on Free Inquiry

THE POLITICAL OUTLOOK of Benedict de Spinoza (1632–77) is much like that of Thomas Hobbes. This is not surprising, for he schooled himself in Hobbes' writings and appropriated most of his ideas from them. Yet on one theme in particular, he exceeded Hobbes: the topic of free inquiry into the nature of things, or as Spinoza described it, the freedom to philosophize and to publish one's thoughts and discoveries. He devoted an entire book to this theme, published in 1670, which he entitled *Theological-Political Treatise*. In it he makes the remarkable claim that this freedom not only does no harm to domestic tranquility and religion, but also that the peace and piety of a society cannot be achieved without it. This is a remarkable claim and deserves close scrutiny, for it contains a valuable lesson.

Spinoza most likely discovered the seed for this claim when reading Hobbes. In Chapter Twelve of *Leviathan*, Hobbes begins his explanation of the origin of religion by observing that we are creatures endowed with a native curiosity. We are especially inquisitive about the causes of things, especially those that may benefit or harm us. From painful experience, we also know that these causes operate without our knowledge or bidding, and that they often cause harm, which can sometimes be catastrophic. And since we do not know when this will happen, we must always be on guard.

Ours, then, is an anxious existence, motivated by fear of what may come, by fear of the unknown. In this anxious state of mind, we imagine causes, powerful unnatural forces, which we personalize, hoping that by offering them homage we might gain their favor and insure ourselves against misfortune. Thus, there arise in human imagination the panoply of Gods, demons, and invisible spirits who are taken to be our guardians or destroyers. Others among us, those of an entrepreneurial spirit, enrich themselves by exploiting the anxieties of others; they become founders of magical or religious cults, over which they claim proprietary rights, and thus grow powerful and rich by the purveying of superstition.

But, besides this, Hobbes perceived that there is another kind of human curiosity, which is disinterested and impartial and not anxious: it is motivated by a purely intellectual desire to know, which leads the mind to conclude after a careful examination of things as they occur that there is a first cause of existence, eternal and infinite, and a supreme power of nature, which is omnipotent and inexhaustible. This is a purely philosophical, impartial, disinterested, and fearless inference. Spinoza adopted it and also the conclusion that underlying everything there is a single irresistible power, an ultimate power of nature, which is the source of everything, and which we may choose to call God. This is a purely intellectual notion of God, unaccompanied by fear or hope, yet seasoned by pure wonder.

I believe that Spinoza pondered over this chapter in *Leviathan* in just this way and was led by it to the signature idea of his philosophical system, that God and Nature are one and the same, and that this supreme and inexhaustible power of being is not a jealous person, who requires worship or expects gratitude, but the ultimate principle of everything, a principle discernible by human reason, which also has the power to explore and explain its ways or operations. In light of this discovery, we learn that the world was not created for our sakes, that our species is an insignificant and most likely temporary presence in the realm of being. The species of material nature are infinite and evolving. The evolution of the human species is a mere moment in the infinite expanse of time.

How does this guarantee peace and piety? If we could question him, I believe Spinoza would answer, "By searching for truth". To his mind, the search after truth, if resolute, becomes an act of pure piety that lifts us out of our petty selves. Truth is an object of respect, and not because we can own it, like riches or power. Truth has no owner. It offers itself to all, always there, the ultimate judge of all our reasonings and judgments concerning it. It requires of us the purest of motives to comprehend it, like a great mountain that sternly challenges fearless climbers, promising no reward but itself. When even a part of it is discovered, that part shows itself in clear and transparent light, like that of the noonday sun. The mind is illuminated, there is no mistaking it. Such discovery is not mysterious. It is the very opposite of mystery; it has an unambiguous clarity, always enlightening. This is the sort of piety unshaped by faith in any historical religion—the types that Spinoza renounced. The truth he envisioned is pure, unsullied, and faultless in fulfilling its promises, favoring no one and accessible to all.

Moreover, a society founded on the principle that free rational inquiry shall not be abridged will be free of internal conflict. It will not be plagued by internal conflicts between zealous advocates of rival orthodoxies, whether religious or secular, or by the machinations of predatory demagogues, because every claim to truth will be subject to rational scrutiny, to a calm and dispassionate inquiry by everyone everywhere—the search for truth becomes everyone's right. This commitment to free inquiry is accompanied and fulfilled by a right and duty of everyone to change their minds whenever they discover their beliefs to be false. They will have learned that nothing trumps truth, the ultimate standard; they honor truth and respect the right of all to seek it. This is the surest means to peace and piety. I believe that Spinoza had it right.

How to Read the Bible
(According to Spinoza)

WHAT IS THE BIBLE? It is a book that contains the sacred scriptures of Judaism and Christianity. However, Jews and Christians differ about its meaning, even though, for the most part, they are referring to much the same thing when they use the name "Bible". A Christian Bible has two parts, whose names "Old Testament" and "New Testament" signify a theological view of human history that I will address shortly.

The first part of the Bible is complete in itself. It comprises the Hebrew Scriptures, or the writings, originally composed in Hebrew, that narrate the history of the ancient Jewish Commonwealth, its rise and fall, and the subsequent exile and dispersal of its people—the Diaspora. Interspersed in the narrative and elaborated in accompanying books are reflections on the fate of the nation and expressions of hope for its reestablishment, since it was believed that God would remain faithful to his promise to Abraham to make of his descendants a great nation. That promise marked the beginning of the nation; of equal importance was the subsequent founding of the Hebrew Commonwealth under Moses, who led the descendants of Jacob, Abraham's grandson, also known as Israel, out of Egypt to the promised land. Moses was not only the founder of the ancient Jewish state, he was also its chief lawgiver and constitutionalist. He was regarded as the greatest of the Hebrew Prophets, for it was believed that he only communicated with God face to face. The founding instruments of the nation and the commonwealth were covenants between God and the people, which promised mutual fidelity without end. The Hebrew Scriptures are far richer in content than this brief outline can convey, and they rightly count among the world's classics.

The New Testament, originally composed in Greek, consists of founding documents of the Christian Church. The name signifies a new covenant, which Christians believed would supersede the covenant with Moses. They believed that Jesus of Nazareth was sent by God to establish a new people, gathered from all the nations of the earth, and that this new nation, called the Church, or Gathering, would replace the nation of Israel as heir to the divine promises made to Abraham and Moses. Like Moses, Jesus was depicted as a lawgiver, and like Moses, he was supposed to have performed miracles to demonstrate his divine vocation. Jesus had another title "Messiah", or "Christ",—that is, the anointed one, or king, whose coming was supposed to be a turning point in the history of the world.

This requires an explanation. A major development in the history of the Jewish Commonwealth was the establishment of a monarchy; as the narrative shows, this was controversial. It led to civil war, which ended with David's triumph and succession to the throne; under his rule and that of his son Solomon, the nation achieved its greatest glory. After this followed a series of misfortunes: civil war, a divided nation, the fall of the monarchy, and exile. Yet out of these misfortunes arose the hope of a future restoration, when God would send a new king, a new David, God's anointed, the Messiah, to restore the nation and revive the kingdom. Early Christians appropriated this "messianic hope", made it their founding idea, and gave it a new meaning. Their chief claim was that Jesus was the divinely anointed Messiah, and that his dominion would know no national boundaries, although it seems from some places in the New Testament that Jesus himself believed his mission was only to "the lost sheep of the house of Israel".

What has this to do with Spinoza? Very much indeed. He was probably the first to practice what has become known as the higher criticism of the Bible. Higher criticism, the study of ancient texts, employs linguistic, literary, and historical methods to recapture the original meaning. It is a secular discipline. The account of the Bible that I gave at the beginning of this essay is a summary of accumulated critical biblical interpretation.

But Spinoza had other interests in addition to historical-critical ones. He wanted to use historical evidence to clarify the relation between theology, politics, and morality, and, by doing so, to draw some important practical conclusions.

To begin with, Spinoza concluded that the Hebrew Bible was basically a political work, whose central narrative was the exodus from Egypt and the founding of the commonwealth under Moses. He supposed that the theological aspects of the narrative are fictional—which is not to say that Moses invented them. Rather he imagined them. Spinoza notes that other nations had similar theological founding myths. To explain this phenomenon, he explores the nature of the prophetic mind. Prophets were biblical personages who received messages from God to deliver to the people. From the prophets' writings, Spinoza concluded that they were persons endowed with an acute moral sensibility and a rich imagination. The combination made them effective communicators, or preachers, able to inspire and lead people. They were not crowd pleasers; their authority derived from their evident moral seriousness and from what they said. Spinoza regarded Jesus and Moses as the best examples of the prophetic vocation, although he also allowed that there are probably instances of this vocation in other cultures.

Spinoza observes that Moses had little to say about divine nature, except that God is eternal and he created order out of chaos at the beginning of the world. This order was taken as evidence that he had "supreme right and power over all things". In sum, the nature of God, as "revealed" in the Scriptures, does not conflict with the philosophical identification of God and Nature. Hence, Spinoza concludes that there is nothing in biblical teaching that would prohibit the freedom to philosophize.

Even more, because of the purity of his moral intuition, Moses was able to conceive a law fit to be a law of nature, for its primary virtues, justice and mercy, were universally acceptable; Moses' successors, the Hebrew prophets, used them to establish a purely moral religion, purged of all sacerdotal rites and sacrifices. The prophet Micah epitomized their achievement in this dialogue between a penitent and a prophet (Micah 6: 6–8):

> "How shall I come before the Lord, and
> bow myself before the high God?
>
> Shall I come before him with burnt
> offerings, with calves of a year old? Will the
> Lord be pleased with thousands of rams, or
> with ten thousands of rivers of oil? Shall I
> give my firstborn for my transgression, the
> fruit of my body for the sin of my soul"?
>
> "He hath showed thee, O man, what is
> good; and what doth the Lord require of
> thee, but to do justly, and to love mercy,
> and to walk humbly with thy God".

Because he found this moral teaching to be eminently rational and an effective means to establish social harmony and peace, Spinoza took these virtues as models of civic virtues, and this moral religion as the standard of civil religion, which stands above and apart from all sectarian religion.

Spinoza's Politics

SPINOZA PERCEIVED POLITICS TO BE AN ART, whose rules derive from experience, and therefore the most reliable resource for a political theory is to be found not in the ideal systems of philosophers and theologians, but in the writings of politicians or their close observers, "for since experience has been their guide, there is nothing they have taught that is remote from practice". It should be clear from the previous essay that Spinoza would include the "writings of Moses" in this class, along with those of Niccolò Machiavelli and Thomas Hobbes, and a host of political histories. He was confident that such authors conversant with political history were able to reveal "every conceivable form of commonwealth... whereby a people may be governed or restrained within fixed bounds". These different forms of government are the results of trial and error. They are, as it were, experimental data.

Political theory should begin with these data and consider which among their set works best in a given situation.

Spinoza observed that human nature is such that no one can "live without a common code of law", but it is also such that everyone puts their own private interest above the interests of others, so that people are, by nature, divided in their loyalties to themselves and to their respective commonwealths. Reconciling these conflicting interests is no simple task, for individual loyalties are by nature passionate, without limit, and unruly. It is not surprising, therefore, that codes of law "have been instituted and public affairs have been conducted by men of considerable intelligence, both astute and cunning".

Cunning and a clear mind are requisite to negotiate between these divided loyalties in order to achieve harmony. Moses, Machiavelli, and Hobbes were taught by experience to be moral pessimists. Moses described the people he was commissioned to lead as "stiff-necked and rebellious". Machiavelli and Hobbes believed that, in general, people are just as likely if not more to be led by passions of individual desire rather than the directives of common reason whose aim is public good.

The art of politics, then, must be able to reconcile private and public interest in a more or less permanent way and to negotiate between natural and civil right. The former is the right of individuals to seek their own advantage; the latter, an imperative to surrender a portion of that right to the commonwealth, to a sovereign power that is independent of all private interests. The former, "Nature's right and established order ... does not frown on strife, or hatred, or anger, or deceit", whereas civil right is a remedy that provides peace and security. But if it is to succeed, it must first establish harmony and gain common consent and approval. Finally, human nature being what it is, the art of politics must devise constitutions that work, whether rulers and subjects are guided by reason or by passion. As has been said, the state must be like a machine that by its constitution runs itself.

Civil society, when it succeeds, is a triumph of worldly intelligence over desire, of the ascendency of reason over the passions. But it is an uncertain victory, for passions persist: envy, greed, ambition, resentment, and jealously never cease.

This pessimistic view of human nature—shared by Moses, Machiavelli, Hobbes, and Spinoza—stands in sharp contrast with utopian viewpoints. Utopians are guided or inspired by a vision of an ideal of society that has never been realized, which is what the word "utopian" means: no place, or nowhere. Utopians suppose that all civil societies are malformed, their governments corrupt and the cause of antisocial passions, whereas human nature is essentially good, awaiting only the perfect regime to be realized. All this, they hope, will be brought about in a revolutionary moment. But Moses, Machiavelli, Hobbes, and Spinoza would see this hope as an illusion.

The ultimate means by which civil society operates is power, a power residing uniquely in the sovereign. This power is "possessed absolutely by whoever has charge of the affairs of state... who makes, interprets, and repeals laws, fortifies cities, makes decisions regarding peace and war". Sovereign power may reside in a council of the people in general, a council of select personages, or in a single individual. Hence, the three standard kinds of civil state: democracy, aristocracy, and monarchy.

Individuals who by their consent subject themselves to a commonwealth have a right to all the advantages that it provides, but they are also bound to obey all of its laws and ordinances, without exception, except when these laws or ordinances can be shown to be unjust. Thus, they are citizens and subjects, but not slaves or servants, for their consent is free and reasonable.

It remains, then to consider the advantages and disadvantages of the three sorts of state. I will be brief, for we have been through them all before with Plato.

Spinoza supposed that a monarchy is a rule of law; thus, even though its laws are decrees by the right of the monarch, there must be consistency and reliability among them, as well as continuity, so that even monarchs, even if absolute rulers, may be called into account for failure to act in conformity to the law. Spinoza cites the laws of the Medes and Persians, which were regarded as eternal, and therefore not subject to the fickleness of a wayward ruler. Moreover, being a monarch comes with duties towards one's realm and one's subjects, and the fulfillment of these duties requires the formation of a government or court made up of wise counselors who possess practical political wisdom.

An aristocracy is also a rule of law, but in this case, laws and their execution are the prerogative of a self-appointed and self-perpetuating council. Thus, consistency and rationality reside here also, but also inordinate privilege of wealth and social standing.

In the end, neither a monarchy nor an aristocracy is adequate in Spinoza's opinion, for in neither of them are those who legislate and execute laws chosen from among all the people. In a democracy, on the other hand, legislators and executives are chosen by law, and no citizen is ineligible to serve in these offices. Only democracy provides for a system of equality of all subjects, all of whom are "in control of their own right".

But here, sadly, Spinoza goes astray. He excludes women and servants, because he sees them as existing under the control of their husbands and their masters. To justify this subjection he writes that "women do not by nature possess equal right with men". And the same would apply to servants. But these exclusions contradict principles of equality and justice that he acknowledged elsewhere—the principle that every individual is unique, that all humans as animate beings possess a common right to exist and persist, as well as a capacity for reason. Indeed, these exclusions contradict his entire philosophical outlook.

JOHN LOCKE

Introducing John Locke

LIKE THOMAS HOBBES, JOHN LOCKE (1632–1704) witnessed civil war and revolution. This happened to him not once but twice. He was a youth during the first English Civil War (1642–49) and came of age during the regency of Oliver Cromwell. In 1660, shortly after the restoration of the English monarchy, he recorded his sentiments of it:

> I no sooner perceived myself in the world, but I found myself in a storm, which has lasted almost hitherto, and therefore cannot but entertain the approaches of a calm with the greatest joy and satisfaction … and do what lies in me to endeavor its continuance, by disposing men's minds to obedience to that government which has brought with it that quiet and settlement which or own giddy folly had put beyond the reach, not only of our contrivance [ability to act], but our hopes.

On the second occasion, Locke was well into his middle age. Once again, the cause of civil unrest was religion. Charles II, whose restoration Locke had celebrated, had no legal heir (although many illegal ones), hence the right of succession resided in his brother James II, who was a Roman Catholic. Parliamentary leaders sought to deprive James of this right; they wanted to establish a Protestant succession. Chief among them, was Anthony Ashley Cooper, the Earl of Shaftesbury, who was Locke's patron and employer. Political crises and war followed.

In 1683, Shaftesbury was forced into exile, and Locke soon followed. He found sanctuary in the Netherlands, whose ruler was William III of Orange, and whose wife, Mary, was the eldest daughter of James II—she had been raised a Protestant. Mary had been James II's presumptive heir until 1688, when James's second wife gave birth to a son, who displaced his elder sister as heir to the throne. So, in 1688, William invaded England and easily defeated the army of James II, who fled the country. William and Mary were invited by Parliament to rule England. This event enabled Locke to end his exile and return to his homeland. Soon after, in 1689, he published *Two Treatises of Government*, his major political work. In the preface, he writes that it was his purpose to offer arguments "sufficient to establish the Throne of our Great Restorer, our present King William; to make good his Title in the Consent of the People ... and to justify to the World, the People of England, whose love of their Just and Natural Rights, saved the Nation when it was on the brink of slavery and ruin". The contrast between Locke's earlier and later comments could not be greater. The former is the speech of a conformist and royalist; in the latter, we hear the voice of a radical and populist. I will attempt to explain this change in a subsequent essay.

In the same year, Locke published a second book, which also brought him fame and recognition. It was entitled, *An Essay Concerning Human Understanding*. It is a long and thoughtful work—over 700 pages in the modern standard edition. Locke began writing it almost twenty years before, in 1671. And, once published, he continued to revise it, bringing out second, third, and fourth editions; he was preparing a fifth edition when he died. It was his life's work.

Its theme is the intellect, or the understanding or mind—he used the terms synonymously. Locke enquires about how the human mind works; how it gathers all of its content; how it arranges this heady content into a rational order; and above all, how it goes about searching after truth. Locke's *Essay* is intended for lovers and adventurers. He likens its narrative to "Hawking and Hunting, wherein the very pursuit makes a great part of the Pleasure"; just as the eye, searching after things, takes pleasure in what it discovers, so the understanding, setting out on a course "to find and follow Truth, will not miss the Hunter's satisfaction". Here, however, the mind's object of pursuit is its very own nature; the task is difficult, unnatural, like the eye trying to observe itself, and therefore the hunt is all the more daring and rewarding. The prize is Truth. Locke wrote his book on behalf of lovers of truth, the pursuit of which is our great adventure.

In the light of the previous essay, the strong connection between Locke's *Essay* and his political writings should be obvious. Locke had read Spinoza and was familiar with Spinoza's claim that the search for truth, the freedom to philosophize, was essential to any well-established civil society. Like Spinoza he believed that it was the basis of true piety, and of peace also, because the truth is something about which all who make honest use of their intellectual faculties can agree on and revere. Truth's decisions end conflicts. They make peace.

But Locke discovered another benefit about the operations of mind that enhance the bonds of civil society. It might be called the joyous contagion of searching after truth. Genuine searches after truth do not indoctrinate, rather they are open invitations to join in the search. After long inquiry, Locke concluded that the mind is a natural thing, connected to an organ of the body. Thinking after truth is a physical action, and the interaction of thinking is like an animal at play, or a trainer letting loose a hawk:

> This, Reader, is the Entertainment of those who let loose their own Thoughts, and follow them in writing; which though thou oughtest not to envy them, since they afford thee an Opportunity of the like Diversion, if thou wilt make use of thy own Thoughts in reading. 'Tis to them, if they are thy own, that I refer myself: But

> if they are taken upon Trust from others,
> 'tis no great matter what they are, they not
> following Truth.

From Locke and Spinoza before him, we may derive this maxim: the only durable and lasting foundation of civil society is Truth, and the search for it, the relentless pursuit, is a duty of all the people and every institution of government. It follows that a primary task of government is to establish public educational institutions that are free and accessible to all.

Does the Mind Always Think?

THIS ESSAY IS NOT ABOUT POLITICS, but the mind. If, as Spinoza and Locke have claimed, the love of truth and a resolute pursuit of it is essential to a healthy and durable civil society, then it becomes necessary to familiarize ourselves with our minds. Locke's *Essay Concerning Human Understanding* is a wonderful resource for this. He asks all the right questions, even though he does not always give the right answers. The pleasure of reading Locke's book derives from discovering what it is to be a rational being.

One of the many questions concerning the mind that Locke explored is posed by the title of this essay: Does the mind always think? Locke's answer is No. He was mistaken, I think. Nevertheless, his reasons are cogent. I will try to explain.

One of the leading questions debated by European philosophers during the 17th century was whether mind and body were two different things; followers of the French philosopher René Descartes argued that mind and body are just that. Mind and body have different essential qualities—an essential quality is a distinguishing characteristic of a thing that makes it the sort of thing that it is. Bodies are all alike, yet different from everything else, by the fact that they occupy space. As Descartes said, they are extended in space. Moreover, no two bodies can occupy the same place, for bodies are also solid. In contrast, minds are not bodies; they are thinking things whose essential quality is thinking. It was further supposed that bodies decay and come apart, whereas minds are simple, indestructible, and immortal—in a word, spiritual. Since the essence of the mind is to think, it would be contradictory to deny that the mind always thinks, as it would be to deny that a body is not extended in space.

Locke disagreed. He believed that mind and body are two aspects of one thing: a human animal. He also believed that human animals are mortal. When they die, they not only lose the capacity to breathe, but also to think. One other conclusion that Locke was led to embrace was that there is no difference between matter and spirit, and that thinking is a capacity that a body, suitably designed, can possess. Like Hobbes and other contemporaries, he believed that the capacity to think resided in the brain.

As evidence against the claim that the mind always thinks, Locke cited the fact that we spend much of our lifetime in deep sleep. Besides, during many of our waking moments our minds seem unoccupied and still, unthinking, without even the trace of a passing fancy. Locke took it as settled that thought and consciousness are necessarily connected. To suppose that we think without being aware of our thoughts is pure nonsense. Now, Locke didn't suppose that we must be conscious of all our thoughts all the time. That would be madness. Thinking involves a measure of self-control; we attend to those thoughts that are relevant, and we disregard others. Still other thoughts are stored by memory, and some we just forget. But even these, if we are reminded of them, we recognize as our own thoughts. And this applies to all our experiences, for thoughts are just aspects of experience.

Locke was a Christian. He believed that when the world ends, the dead shall be raised, and the secrets of all hearts shall be revealed at the last judgment. He also believed that no one can be judged for thoughts and actions that they cannot own, which is to say, cannot remember. Being able to own one's thoughts and actions is being a responsible person.

One of the most studied sections in Locke's Essay concerns what it is to be a person. He posed the question:

how does one know oneself to be the same person? How do I know when I awake in the morning that I am the same person I was when I fell asleep last night? Or, how do I know, when I recall some childhood event, that it was I who caused it or was the object of it? Locke's answer to all these questions is the same: consciousness. It is my consciousness of being myself that makes me the same person. We are creatures who know ourselves and come into possession of ourselves over time, a feat accomplished through consciousness. The capacity to own oneself over time makes one the same person, and also the same moral being, for by owning oneself and one's past actions, a person takes responsibility for them.

Now, I believe that in all of this Locke is right. Yet I also think that he was mistaken in supposing that the mind does not always think. If he was mistaken, then thinking and the consciousness of thinking are not coextensive. In other words, sometimes we think and don't know it. Experience supports this hypothesis. More often than not, I find that I do my best thinking when asleep. That often I will fall asleep with a problem that I cannot resolve, and I will awake in the middle of the night, greeted by a flood of thoughts and words, then by a moment of wonderful clarity. As though the mind were at work all the while, sifting through thoughts and experiences. Here, I am reminded once more of Hobbes: the mind is a physical thing, an organ, that works even when we are not aware of it working, and thinking is a sort of counting, or ongoing computational process that takes place in the brain and nervous system. To be sure, when I awake into these lucid moments, moments of wonderful enlightenment and discovery, I recognize that these thoughts are mine. But these thoughts are more than mine. Some of them have the aspect of truth and seem to direct my mental focus to a place outside my mind and a recognition of how things really are.

One requires Spinoza to top off any thinking about thought that arises after reading Hobbes and Locke. Perhaps, as he supposed, there is a universal intelligence, not a divine creator, but rather an order of things, like laws of nature, which regulate everything and gives them a coherent totality, which is Nature. This is not a personal God. Rather it is the nature of things, which we discover through patient inquiry.

Locke Against Patriarchy

PATRIARCHY IS VILE, LIKE AN INVASIVE WEED that has taken root in all human institutions: the family, the state, churches, and most of professions. Perfect equality will not be achieved until it is rooted out completely and cast aside as such. In many ways, it is comparable to the practice of slavery, which it mimics. If one were seeking reasons to honor John

Locke, one is sure to find that here, for he was the first man to oppose patriarchy publicly.

Having reviled it, I am obliged to define it. By "patriarchy", I do not mean fatherhood in general, which coupled with motherhood, forms the essential social institution of parenthood. Patriarchy is a social and political doctrine, drawing upon the belief that fathers have an absolute right to rule their families as they see fit. This right of dominion is supposed to range over wives and children and includes the right of life and death. Advocates of patriarchy believed that civil government is an instance of paternal power and authority. They supposed that monarchy is the only proper form of government, and that only men are rightfully monarchs, while those whom they rule, their subjects, are children. And of course, "Father knows best". The patriarchal state was supposed to be like a great family, in which children never progress to mature adulthood, nor women beyond servitude.

This doctrine became fashionable in England during the 17th century and was popularized by a now largely forgotten political writer, Sir Robert Filmer, in a book entitled *Patriarcha, or The Natural Power of Kings*.

Filmer claimed that the doctrine of patriarchy is grounded in divine revelation and recorded in the Bible. He claimed that Adam, the first man, is the archetypal monarch and representative of the species, or more specifically, the male half of it. He noted that, according to the biblical narrative, after God created Adam, he granted him sovereignty over the whole of earth, commanding him to "be fruitful, multiply, fill the earth, and subdue it". The creation of Eve was an afterthought; it gave Adam, the man, a sexual partner and helper.

Adam's sovereignty was supposed to be transmitted to all of his male heirs, which could happen in several ways: directly from father to son, or if a father had several sons, he could divide his dominion and grant a part to each of them, as Noah did for Shem, Ham, and Japheth, granting each a different portion of the earth. Or a kingdom could be acquired by usurpation, as David did. By whatever means, and however many kingdoms there came to be, a king's power was supposed to be supreme and undivided within his dominion. For all other human beings, male and female were not born free and equal, rather as subjects and servants. However, every male had the consolation of being lord of his particular household, his little domain. So much for patriarchy.

Enter Locke. His major political work is entitled *Two Treatises of Government*. First published in 1689, it was composed almost a decade earlier. As the title states, the book contains two parts, which were originally planned as the beginning and concluding chapters of a much longer work; regrettably, the missing parts have been lost.

Locke takes on Filmer in the *First Treatise*. His refutation is long and tedious, but it is worth reading, for it contains some very enlightened biblical interpretation. For example, writing on Genesis 1: 27–8, Locke offers this crucial passage:

> So God created man in his own image, in
> the image of God created he him; male and
> female created he *them*. And God blessed
> *them*, and said to *them*, Be fruitful, and
> multiply and fill the earth and subdue it,
> and have dominion over the fish of the
> sea, and the fowl of the air, and over every
> living thing that moveth upon the earth.

Now, Locke observes, rightly I believe, that God's command to be fruitful and multiply is not addressed to a particular man, named Adam, but to the species of mankind, whose basic unit is binary: male and female. God addressed both together, and through them all their successive generations. Note that the Hebrew word adam, is not a proper name, but denotes a species, like eagle, or rabbit, or horse. This dominion, then, is granted to the entire species, which consists of male and female members—an essential feature of mankind, for without it there could be no generation and no future, without which, the divine directive would have been idle. It is only in Genesis 2 that an individual man appears. Even there, he is not called by name, but referred to as "the man". From a literary-critical perspective, Genesis 1 and 2 are entirely separate narratives, which cannot be harmonized—but this is going beyond Locke.

And what sort of dominion did God grant to the human species in Genesis 1? Locke notes that it has nothing to do with government or sovereignty. God did not make Adam "Monarch of the earth". Rather, he granted mankind the use of the earth and all other living things as means to sustain life. It was supposed to be a grant in common of the earth and its resources to all in common, male and female, in their successive generations; it consisted of a right to hunt and fish and till the soil and to build habitations made from stone and timber and other material resources.

Filmer also claimed that the doctrine of male sovereignty was supported by the fifth commandment. Here, too, Locke is right that Filmer has misread the text, for the commandment does not say, "Honor thy father", but "Honor thy father and thy mother". Moreover, Locke observes that the commandment does not enjoin that children regard their parents as absolute rulers, but that they show them proper respect. The structure of the family was not meant to be a paradigm for civil government. Nor were parents' power over their children absolute. Locke insists that the authority of parents over their children extends only to the period of their immaturity; it is more properly parental care, which is supposed to nourish and prepare a child for life. Once a child attains maturity, that role ends. What is left when all goes well is gratitude and deep affection.

Locke concludes his argument by affirming this principle: man, the species, and hence male and female, are created free and equal; they possess the earth in common. This is the thesis upon which Locke will build his theory of civil government and offer explanations of how, from this common endowment, or state of nature, individuals, societies, and nations can gain exclusive right to parts of it—how, that is to say, not only life and liberty but also property are to be acquired and secured.

The Origin of Civil Society

How DID CIVIL SOCIETY or the civil state begin? There is general agreement that a civil state is not a product of nature, but of human art, the art of politics. This is what Hobbes believed and affirmed in the memorable sentence that begins his great work, *Leviathan*: "Nature (the Art whereby God made and governs the World) is by the Art of man, as in many other things, so in this also imitated, that it can make an Artificial Animal".

The great animal which he then describes is the civil state. He likens its parts to the parts of the human body: sovereignty is its soul or vital principle, public officials are its joints, laws its sinews, rewards and punishments its nerves, the welfare of the people its chief business. He gave the state a fearsome name: Leviathan. He did not suppose that this act of creation happened only once but many times over; it was ongoing and continuous. Locke agreed.

But if we human beings are mere animals, and civil states are artificial creatures made by us, then the question arises, what is it about us and our circumstances that makes us want to make such things? Remember that the civil state is only one of the many sorts of things created by human art. Among them: clothing, houses, and all their furnishings, ploughs, the wheel, saws, and axes, musical instruments, and lethal weapons. The will to survive is the general cause of all this creative activity. But there are other causes too, such as having the means for living comfortably and well, convenience in meeting needs, efficiency in assuring our safety, and having at hand instruments of sheer delight to occupy our moments of leisure and to enhance our comfort.

What originally prompted mankind to create the civil state and how did it all come about? Hobbes' answer is 'to make peace,' for the state of nature is a state of war of all against all, and, given our selfish and aggressive nature, we are never free of becoming victims of it. To this end, it was necessary that a formal agreement or covenant or social contract be enacted between people, a union of wills. Locke, on the other hand, agreed with the method but disagreed on the reason. He did not believe that the state of nature is a state of war. To his mind, war is just one more thing that mankind has made, and, whether it be civil war or a war between nations, it presupposes the existence of states or nations. I should take note before proceeding further that Locke's account of the origin of civil society is given in *The Second Treatise of Government*, which bears the title *An Essay Concerning the True Original, Extent, and End of Civil Government*.

Some interpreters of Locke believe that he had a softer and more sentimental view of human nature than Hobbes. They are mistaken. *The Second Treatise* is not at all sentimental. In fact, in some places, Locke's remarks seem downright cruel. He differs from Hobbes regarding the place of law in the nature of things.

If the state of nature is a state of war, then it must be a totally lawless state, for war was considered to be absent of all law. Hence, the saying "All's fair in love and war". But Locke believed this is impossible, for he was sure that every human being is a bearer of the law of nature, whose content includes the whole of public morality—especially keeping one's word, for without that there could be no social contract.

According to Locke, the state of nature is one of perfect equality, in which all human beings are free "to order their Actions, and dispose of their Possessions, and Persons" as they please, without "depending on the Will of any other Man". Yet they are always "within the bounds of the Law of Nature", for human nature is endowed with this law, and in a state of nature, every human being is not only a bearer of this law but has executive power to apply it. The law can be harsh. If anyone assaults me, I have the right to kill him; if a thief enters my house, I have the same right. And, Locke adds, if my condition is secure, I should consider it my duty "to preserve the rest of Mankind" and to do whatever tends "to the Preservation of the Life, Liberty, Health, Limb, or Goods of another", if need be by using the same harsh methods, treating thieves as one would dangerous beasts of the wild. It is hard to distinguish this vigilante justice from the state of war of all against all. They are equally suited to the Wild West. In Locke's case, the reason for founding a civil state is to create an orderly administration of law, which is not so different from making peace.

But there are more important differences between Locke and Hobbes, which pertain to the notion of sovereignty. Hobbes believed that sovereignty properly belongs to governors, whether they be many or one. Locke disagreed; he located sovereignty in the people.

Hobbes maintained that those who rule, whether a monarch or a representative assembly, are above the law; for the law is an expression of their arbitrary will. Locke, to the contrary, contended that rulers have an absolute duty to promote the welfare of the people, and in any case are just as much subject to the law as anyone under their rule. Monarchs who violate this rule by seeking their own advantage rather than the welfare of the people lose their legitimacy and become tyrants, and the people, every one of which is a bearer of the law, have the right to remove them.

But this right must be carefully defined. Locke did not conceive it as a right to revert to a state of nature, for the people who have once given their consent, directly or tacitly, to the formation of a civil society cannot dissolve that society. They can do no more than replace the government. Locke does not spell out the process, but he seems to imply something like a constitutional convention, enacted by the people through their special representatives, who would temporarily assume powers of government: executive, legislative, and judicial.

Here, I think, the very idea of the rule of law comes into view with all its power, and we should pay close attention. For it seems today that members of our civil society have many grievances, some just, some unjust, but in either case, their preferred method of dealing with them more often than not is to go outside the law and become instruments of violence and anarchy. It is like throwing out the baby with the bathwater.

So, here's the problem. Given human nature, and its universal tendency to be corrupted by power, grievances must come. How are those who are aggrieved to seek redress within the rule of law? Locke posed the problem but failed to provide a reliable solution. I believe that the framers of our constitution provided one. There is more to come.

Private Property

Locke believed that the paramount duty of civil government is to safeguard the life, liberty, and property of all the people. However, a person's right to these things is not a civil right, but a right of nature, that is, an inalienable human right; it becomes also a civil right for anyone who consents to enter a civil state.

The right to life and liberty begins and ends with existence. We are all born free. But, in a state of nature, we enter the world without any property at all, except our bodies and our selves; they are our native property—hence, slavery is not only wrong but unnatural. Moreover, in a state of nature, the earth belongs to everyone in common. But since all persons have a right to preserve themselves in being, this right extends to the use of everything that the earth provides that can be used for our subsistence, safety, and comfort. If the earth belongs to all in common, then how does a part of it become mine and not another's?

This is Locke's answer: the labor involved in appropriating some part of the earth makes that particular part our own. If, in a state of nature, I pick an apple from a tree, or, like a squirrel, gather acorns that have fallen to the ground, or scoop a pot of water from a running stream, all these are mine, for all these involve some physical effort.

This method of accumulation applies to the earth itself. In a state of nature, where all is common, by tilling the soil and planting a garden, I make that portion of earth my own (so long as another has not tilled it first), because I have mixed my labor with it. Scholars credit Locke with having invented, or discovered, the labor theory of property. Whatever anyone acquires by their own labor becomes theirs—they own it, it is their property, but with the proviso that this applies only so long as they leave enough for others, and that what is left is as good as what they have taken: "He that leaves as much as another can make use of, does as good as take nothing at all".

There is another proviso: In my little plot of soil, I may grow only so much as I can use; I must not be wasteful or produce so much that a large portion will spoil. Nature prohibits wastefulness of a common resource, no matter how abundant it is. And as sign of this, Locke argues, God made it happen that the excess of any harvest would soon spoil, and so could not be kept.

Locke imagined that this is what it was like before the earth was as populated as it is now. He imagined that the so-called "New World" was like this: "In the beginning all the World was America, and more so than it is now; for no such thing as Money was anywhere known".

What changes did the invention of money bring? Suppose that Methuselah and his wife were tillers of the soil (Genesis 25–7). All things were in common, and there was plenty for all, but under Locke's proviso, they could grow no more than they could use. Yet Methuselah lived so long (969 years) that we may imagine he developed into a very skillful tiller of the soil, and so often likely produced harvests greater than he could use. What to do with the excess? He could give some away, or he could barter for products he did not grow: trade brussels sprouts for plums, and so forth. Then suppose that he was offered in trade pieces of shiny gold metal, which were not edible, but had the advantage of being imperishable, not to mention shiny and pleasing to the eye; they could be accumulated without fear of corruption and decay.

Somehow the idea popped into someone's head that these pieces of metal could be used as standard instruments of trade—as money—which allowed Methuselah to acquire more wealth and more land, to produce more, and trade it for more shining metal. Locke imagines that this is how industry and commerce began. He does not seem to have been bothered by the rise of great estates and fortunes, by boundless acquisitiveness and the exploitation of the landless, as were Plato and the Biblical prophets.

Locke also invented the labor theory of value: it was through the industry of those who tilled the land that its value increased, and he compared developed Europe with undeveloped America, which, he supposed, was a mere wilderness, where the land was free for the taking, but only by lawful monarchs. He observed that while the value of this freely acquired land was increased by those who cultivated it, ownership did not accrue to these tillers of the land, for Locke believed that one could sell one's labor to another, and with it the right of ownership over what they produced and its value. Thus, those who owned the land and other resources, and the money to finance their use and development, could grow enormously rich, whereas those whose labor produced things, who tilled the soil and endowed it with value, were relegated to the status of day-laborers. These day-laborers received as wages only a minuscule portion of the value that their labor produced.

Now, all of this leads to still another way to acquire property, which involves no labor at all. Any wilderness was considered free for the taking, if one was a lawful monarch. Having helped themselves to it, such a monarch could give portions of the land away to their favored subjects, as grants. Locke makes no mention of this practice in his political writings, but he was a beneficiary of it. Among his unpublished manuscripts is a document entitled "The Fundamental Constitutions of Carolina"; it is a draft constitution for the Carolina Colony, consisting of a vast territory including what is now the states of North and South Carolina and much of Georgia. This territory was a grant to eight nobles in the English court. Chief among them was Locke's patron and employer, the Earl of Shaftesbury. As Shaftesbury's private secretary, Locke was the principal drafter of the "Constitutions".

The document is dated July 21st, 1669 and begins with the declaration of Charles II, King of England, granting the territory to the "Lords Proprietors" as their hereditary possession, or fiefdom. The territory could be further subdivided, and additional grants made. Locke was a recipient of one of them. These were ennobling grants, so that Locke also acquired the title of Landgrave, a title he never used, preferring to be called "Gentleman". Later he sold the property, and perhaps with it went the title. What is noteworthy of the constitution is that it is more feudal than modern. The colony has a government—a council and courts of justice. But these bodies are established from above. There is no mention of a social contract. I will not describe it further; anyone interested may find it online.

The constitutions raise questions about Locke's liberalism, and indeed about his modernity, for he was considered a founder of both. I will consider these questions in the next essay.

Liberalism and the Meaning of History

Was John Locke a liberal? There seems to be a consensus among scholars that he was, but only in a very limited sense. It all depends on what one means by "liberal", and, because it means many things, one must take each meaning in turn.

A liberal believes in human equality and the right of individuals to think what they will, to rely on their own judgments concerning truth and falsehood, right and wrong, and to be the absolute owners of themselves, their persons and their bodies. They must be the ultimate deciders of their own fate and fortune—although I should add here, "God willing", for as a Christian and theist, Locke believed that God owned and decided everything.

In any case, it's very clear that Locke believed these things. He based his case for religious toleration on them. He argued that belief, religious or otherwise, is an individual affair and, if it is to be genuine and sincere, it cannot be coerced. Because coercion cannot change belief, but only what is outwardly professed, it would be wrong to attempt torture, for that approach would cause insincerity. Any government authority to adopt that approach would be unjust. It would, in effect, employ torture to compel innocent persons to confess to crimes they didn't commit. For the same reason, Locke advocated the complete separation of Church and State. It is up to each individual to decide what to believe and what form of religion to practice.

He was, however, an imperfect advocate of these liberal ideas. Unlike Spinoza, he did not advocate unrestricted freedom of inquiry, the pursuit of truth wherever it led. He condemned Spinoza because Spinoza equated God with Nature and denied divine providence. Locke wrote that a civil society is not obligated to tolerate anyone who holds such beliefs.

Also, Locke did not champion women's rights, even though he believed that in a state of nature, men and women are equal. Locke's closest friend was a woman, Damaris Lady Masham. They were Platonic lovers for almost a quarter of a century. Not long after Locke returned to England from exile, he became a permanent resident at her husband's country estate where they lived together as intellectual partners. Lady Masham was an advocate of women's right to education, arguing that if men were going to entrust women with the early education of their sons, they should want them to have gone to school. She also wrote two books, published anonymously. The ideas expressed in them are similar to Locke's, and it has often been supposed that he influenced her thinking. But it could just as well have been that she influenced him—I'm sure she did. As I have noted, they were intellectual partners.

Notwithstanding his commitment to freedom and equality as a natural right, Locke countenanced slavery, which is a plain contradiction of his principles. He accepted its practice in the American colonies. So much for the consistency of great thinkers!

Economic liberals believe in free trade and a free market. Locke did not. He was a mercantilist, which is to say that he favored national regulation of the supply of money and the quality of the coin of the realm, and also the regulation of foreign trade to the advantage of national industries, especially textiles. He favored colonization as a means of economic growth and slavery as a source of affordable labor. Furthermore, he did not worry, as did the ancients, about the accumulation of great wealth in the hands of the few. He desired full employment and was interested in measures that would put the able-bodied idle poor to work, but under conditions that looked more like servitude than freedom of opportunity. His references to day laborers in his writings show that he was more concerned about their prospects for getting into heaven than receiving a fair and livable wage.

Liberals believe in unlimited economic progress. Locke did not. Although he believed in human equality and the possibility of unlimited economic growth, he did not apply these beliefs to history. He expected that world history would end sometime during the 18th century, a conclusion based on his study of the Bible. During the last decade of his life, Locke received frequent visits from Isaac Newton. They were friends, although not intimate ones. The purpose of these visits was to read and discuss the Bible, especially the book of Revelation, in which they believed was foretold the second coming of Christ and the end of history, to be followed by a thousand-year reign of Christ on earth—although on this last point Locke was undecided. In any case, Locke believed that God would abruptly end the course of history. The dead would be raised, and there would be a final judgment of all mankind, and a final separation of the sheep from the goats. Then, the old world would be destroyed to make way for a new heaven and earth, which would be everlasting.

The idea of unlimited social and economic progress did not gain currency, and was perhaps not even conceived, until the 18th century. The revolutions across the globe of the 18th, 19th, and early 20th centuries were initiated with such ends in view. A more peaceful version of this idea also was established in the very character of Western Civilization, and the possibility of it was clarified, and its probability increased, by the industrial revolution and the rapid growth of technology. The United States of America became the principal guardian and administrator of the idea of progress, of the pursuit of a secular millennium, and it was believed that our nation was destined to guide the rest of the world to its ultimate realization.

After the Cold War ended, some prophets of secular history have proposed that history reached its end. They did not declare the end of time and with it all change; rather they declared that human society, through a long process of trial and error, had finally achieved its most reliable and durable forms, social, political, and economic. Whatever setbacks may occur thereafter, they would not change the settled course of history—rather they would be followed by greater freedom, equality, and economic wellbeing.

This is a nice idea. But it is barely more credible than the religious fantasies entertained by Locke, Newton, and their intellectual friends. And, I am sure, it is the wrong idea to have in mind as we turn to consider the political meaning of the U.S. Constitution and the intellectual motives and goals of its principal framers.

DIDEROT

Diderot's Political Naturalism

OF ALL THE GREAT personages of the Enlightenment, Denis Diderot (1713–84) is probably the most modern. His opinions anticipate all of modern liberalism; the founders of this country were schooled in his thought. Like John Locke, he was a philosophical naturalist, a materialist, a proponent of natural science, but, unlike Locke, he was also an atheist, a proponent of the secular state and of a secular morality to go with it. Not to mention an advocate of free love and gender equality, a cultural relativist, and a defender of religious toleration and of freethinking. He was also an opponent and harsh critic of colonialism and of its notorious consequences, namely, slavery and economic exploitation, calling attention to their ill effects on non-European society and culture. He was the first writer to explore what he considered to be the inevitable entanglement of Christianity with sexuality, and its unhappy psychological effects, and the first to describe the tragic consequences of this: unbearable guilt, sadomasochistic cruelty, and madness. He describes these conditions with great empathy and concern.

Diderot gained fame not so much as an author but as an editor. He edited the *Encyclopédie*, the great French Encyclopedia of the Sciences, Arts, and Crafts, a multi-volumed work that became a monument of the age, a treasury of enlightened learning. Thus, he is more often thought of as an enabler of the Enlightenment than as one of its major figures, like Rousseau or Voltaire. In consequence, his writings are often ignored, even though his writing shows him to be a more acute thinker. Furthermore, his philosophical and critical writings are mostly in the form of articles—many written for the *Encyclopédie*, fragmentary and scattered over a broad range of subjects. He left his readers with the task of unifying his thoughts.

There is, I believe, a common theme, or point of view, that unites them, and it is central to modern liberalism: his empirical naturalism. This theme is evident in almost all his writings, in his choice of topics, and what he wrote about them. I will try to illustrate this by commenting on two short works, one entitled "Letter on the Blind for the Use of those who can see", and the other, an article on natural right written for the *Encyclopédie*.

Diderot's "Letter on the Blind" consists of reflections on a theme that may seem very remote from politics. It concerns what has come to be known as "the Molyneaux Problem", a hypothetical question posed by William Molyneaux in a letter to John Locke dated July 7th, 1688. Molyneaux was concerned with the truth of Locke's claim that all the ideas that occupy our minds originate from sensory experience. Now, suppose a man born blind were to have his sight restored: the practice of the surgical removal of cataracts was just beginning. Here is the problem as Locke summarized it:

> Suppose a Man born blind, and now adult, and taught by his touch to distinguish between a Cube, and a Sphere of the same metal, and nearly of the same bigness, so as to tell, when he felt one and the other; which is the Cube, which the Sphere. Suppose then the Cube and Sphere placed on a Table, and the Blind Man to be made to see [i.e. his sight surgically restored]. I ask, Whether by his sight, before he touched them, he could now distinguish, and tell, which is the Globe, which the Cube.

Molyneaux thought he could not, and, after some hesitation, Locke agreed; the once blind man, now with his sight restored, would first have to learn from experience that sight and touch concur. It is a fascinating problem and probably is still unsolved. Molyneaux's question has drawn the attention of neuroscientists to this day.

Diderot enlarges the question to include moral ideas and sentiments. The Enlightenment is commonly described as the Age of Reason, but it was equally an age of feeling, a sentimental age. This was, after all, also the age of Grand Opera. Diderot believed that moral rules are lacking in effect without empathy, the deep sensibility for others. For example, the Golden Rule, "Do unto others, as you would have others do unto you" would have little effect unless we had some sense for the feelings of others. In this connection, he believed that the face is the most expressive part of the body, even more than the voice—the sounds of laughter, cries, or screams—and that among facial features, nothing is more expressive than the eyes themselves as instruments revealing a whole variety of human emotions: joy, hatred, and fear; anguish, boredom, contempt, and more.

Even apart from the face, the mere bulk of another living animal affects us, although that affect appears to diminish with the animal's size: "we feel for a horse in pain and squash an ant without giving it a moment's notice". The moral sentiments do not originate in the inner sanctum of our self, rather we learn them from seeing others, and there develops a concurrence between what we see in others and what we feel for ourselves. Here, he supposed, is the origin in nature of moral sentiments and of morality. And because justice, a moral principle, is a fundamental principle of politics, politics must have the same origin.

What of the man born blind who cannot see the faces of others or the expressions of an animal writhing in pain? He is not without feelings, and because he does not live as a hermit, but in society with others, he develops capacities that seem to those who have vision to be remarkable in sensitivity and discernment: his sense of place, of direction, of order, especially the mathematical order of things. Diderot remarks that a person born blind can develop through touch a sense of symmetry, but not of beauty. Yet, he conjectures, pity may be less well developed in those born blind just because they cannot see the faces of others. On the other hand, such individuals have greater self-mastery and are less inclined to self-pity because living in a world shaped by people with sight, they are always reminded of their deprivation. This may seem paradoxical. But it is not. All of these ideas remain open questions, like Molyneaux's problem. Still, these hypotheses may put beyond doubt our great dependence on the senses for information—information without which our moral senses would not develop, or must develop in a different way.

How does this all relate to the origin of civil society? Diderot agrees with Rousseau; the individual must be transformed into a citizen. This transformation must be an act of each individual acting on their rational choice. Diderot's account of how this transformation takes place is striking in its originality: every one of us is faced with a choice between pure selfishness and conforming our will to the will of the whole.

Diderot imagines the selfish person to be at war with the human race, for he desires all praise, all riches, all grand attributes for himself—much like a selfish child whose every want is satisfied on demand, and whose demands persist even when they become adults and hold high, or even the highest, public office. Others quite properly regard such an egoistic person with indignation and scorn. But their revulsion is warranted only as an expression of a universal will: the will of a society of persons who choose to live under a universal law that applies to everyone in the same way and with the same rigor, a law that is just only if it is applied with equity to all.

Diderot on Duty and Justice

DENIS DIDEROT'S FATHER, DIDIER DIDEROT, was a master craftsman, a maker of fine cutlery and surgical instruments, but he had higher ambitions for his children. His desire was that they enter the Church, and he was disappointed when Denis, the eldest, chose rather to study law; his disappointment increased when Denis abandoned the legal profession and became a writer. On top of all this his son became a professing atheist. Denis's younger brother, however, followed his father's wishes and ultimately became an archdeacon, while a sister, Angelique, joined a sisterhood of nuns. Yet despite their differences, affection between father and son remained strong, so much so that it was rumored the father favored him over his clerical son. Diderot's affection and respect are evident in a short story in which he memorializes his father. He entitled it "Conversation of a Father with His Children".

The narrative presents the father, now old and in poor health, reflecting on his life. He had probated wills and settled estates and did so with such care and integrity that he was held in high reputation as an honest man, his services much in demand. Commenting on the dangers faced by anyone reputed to be "a man of principle", he adds, "Would you believe, my children, there was a moment when I was on the verge of ruining you—yes, utterly ruining you", which evoked the eager response, "How Papa?".

And so he tells this story: an aged priest had died, and Diderot's father—all the characters in Diderot's stories are drawn from those he knew in his life—was asked by his relatives to settle his estate. The relatives were very poor, presenting "the most hideous spectacle of poverty you could hope to see", and expected that their poverty was about to be relieved. Charity compelled the father to accept their plea: "How could I refuse to paupers a service I had done for so many wealthy families"? It turned out, in a twist, that the priest had amassed a fortune, a hundred thousand francs, equivalent perhaps to one million dollars in today's currency. Making an inventory of the dead priest's tangible goods, the father discovered a strongbox under the floor boards, which seemed to contain only "useless stuff": letters, receipts, expense lists. All discarded. The strongbox had no cover, which suggested that it also had been discarded. Yet, in the box, beneath these "useless" papers, Diderot's father found a will that appeared to have been written long ago. The executors named in it had been dead for twenty years. He read the will, and was disheartened. The will left nothing to the natural heirs, but everything to a rich bookseller in Paris.

The father was alone in the priest's house and seated by a fire. He despaired over what he had just read. He read the will over and over, and it became more and more odious to him, because it was unjust. He thought, "What am I to do? I am seated near the fire. Shall I burn it?". He held it out toward the fire, drew it back; he repeated this gesture over and over again.

What made him hesitate? He was sure the will would cause a great injustice—not to mention anguish, disappointment, and misery among the heirs. On the other hand, this additional wealth would mean nothing to the designated legatee. But the will was clear, and he felt obliged to honor it. His vocation required that he do so. His reputation depended on it. Yet he worried that by honoring the will he would be responsible for a great injustice.

He remained awake all night, seated by the fire, pondering what to do. The next morning, he left the house, and sought the advice of a well-known casuist, a learned priest, Father Bouin.

Here, there is a break in the father's story. The family doctor pays a visit to check on the health of the father, who inquires after the physician's other patients, one in particular, a former mayor of the town. This former mayor is a scoundrel, who was tried and convicted of embezzling. Subsequently, he became critically ill, yet nonetheless, the doctor is confident that he can save him. This draws from the father the remark that this would be a disservice to the patient and to the public, for the gallows awaits him, and, besides, "there are enough scoundrels in the world". The doctor responds, "My business is to heal people, not to judge them", and if, by healing a man, I only save him for the hangman, so be it.

The father resumes his tale. He visits Father Bouin, the casuist, who exhorts him to do exactly what the will dictates. When the father objects, the casuist scolds him. What authority has he to do otherwise? Can he interpret the mind of the dead priest? Can he take his place? No. "No one has the right to infringe the law or to read the mind of the dead or dispose of his property". The father's duty is clear, and he must do it. Returning from his visit to the priest, he wondered to himself what if he had destroyed the will, as he had been tempted to do? He would have been obliged to pay the bequest himself, and this would have ruined him financially.

On his return, the father carefully locks up all the valuables. The dead priest's would-be heirs are awaiting him anxiously. He calls them in: "There I was, pale as death, trembling, opening my mouth and shutting it again, beginning sentences I could not finish, weeping". But finally, the words come out: "A will, a will which disinherits you". What follows is a scene he shudders to recount. "I can see them now: some rolling on the ground, tearing their hair; some gouging their cheeks and breasts; some foaming at the mouth and swinging their children by the feet, ready to dash their skulls on the pavement if not prevented".

The designated legatee appears. The father's one last hope was that this very rich man, having no need of an inheritance, would take pity on the poor relatives. His very appearance suggested that he would not. "Great shaggy black eyebrows, tiny furtive eyes, a big mouth with a twist in it, and a pock marked face". And, in fact, he did not.

When his father has finished his tale, Diderot upbraids him. "Duty required you listen to your heart, which has been in pain ever since". Granted that, had he destroyed the will, his father would have been obliged to pay the legatee out of his own resources, but for the same reason, having followed the dictates of the will, was he not likewise obliged to pay the rightful heirs what they deserved? His father asks him to drop the subject. It is too painful to continue.

Diderot wrote this narrative, part memory, part fiction, for a philosophical purpose, to illustrate a dilemma that we all confront from time to time between duty and justice—the former a clear and compelling mandate, the latter a sentiment, no less compelling. It reveals a divided impulse of the moral will: the one conservative, the other liberal, which shows that the divide between liberal and conservative is within us, just as it is all around us.

Diderot's Religion

In the previous essay, I mentioned that Diderot was a professing atheist. And yet his mind harbored something very much like a religious sentiment. He was quite aware of this, and aware also of the irony of it, but it did not trouble him. Suffice it to say that, by claiming to be an atheist, Diderot dismissed all the claims to truth of historical or organized religions as fantasy and error, but that did not exclude him from having religious sentiments.

His religious sentiment finds expression in a story he wrote entitled "D'Alembert's Dream". Jean Le Rond d'Alembert (1717–83) was Diderot's friend, co-editor with him of the Enclopedié, and a leading mathematician. The characters of Diderot's fictional works were all persons known to him, which explains why he hesitated to publish them. Instead he circulated his stories in manuscript form. Fiction was his preferred means of exploring philosophical questions.

"D'Alembert's Dream" consists of three parts, ranging over a variety of themes, metaphysical and moral. The second and third parts deal with human gender and sexuality—and remain very pertinent today. Yet the first, which is metaphysical and no less pertinent, is the subject of this essay.

Metaphysics is the study of the real nature of things. Metaphysical discourse is about what there is, not singly, but as a whole. Diderot regarded nature as the totality of everything that is, a vital system constantly evolving. The first part of "D'Alembert's Dream" opens with a short account of his belief. I present this in his own words (although in translation), for no paraphrase would do it justice:

> Nature is a Being who exists somewhere
> but corresponds to no one point in space,
> a Being with no dimensions yet occupying
> space, who is complete in himself at every
> point in this space, who differs in essence
> from matter, who is moved by matter
> and moves matter but never moves itself,
> who acts upon matter yet undergoes all
> its changes, a Being of whom I have no
> conception whatever, so contradictory is
> it by nature....

The irony of this definition of nature is that it is reminiscent of theological definitions of God. This is what Diderot intended, for like Spinoza before him, he wanted to replace theology with a philosophy of nature, and like Spinoza, he offered proof of it—although, unlike Spinoza, not through abstract arguments. Instead he presented nature concretely, materially, and naturally.

Diderot's definition of nature is a set of oppositions: Nature is everywhere and nowhere; it is extended in space and yet not extended, for it is complete at every point; it is not matter yet it undergoes all the changes that matter undergoes; it is moved yet never moved; and, finally, this concept of nature is not a mere concept, because the natural sciences contain the proof of the totality of nature.

What does all this mean? His object is nature, and nature is basically a material, generative substance. Diderot derived his materialism from Lucretius; it is a form of atomism. He believed that the universe was the product of the random movement of atoms colliding in space. But unlike Lucretius, he supposed the basic particles of matter possessed something else, a force or "energy" (an Aristotelian term that was just then receiving a new modern meaning) that made the particles capable of generating everything: inorganic material bodies, plants, animals, and beings like us, who have the ability to think and speak, and who are conscious of ourselves over time. Hence, moral persons. The power of the atom is generative of all these things, which do not exist individually, but are joined in an ever-renewing totality, the universe. Diderot's vision of nature is vast and without limit. It is sublime, for to contemplate nature elevates the mind and fills it with joyous wonder. This sublime sense of nature comprised Diderot's religion. He needed nothing more to satisfy his ultimate concern.

The first part of "D'Alembert's Dream" is a dialogue between Diderot and D'Alembert. Having presented his object, the totality of nature, Diderot proceeds to offer proof of it. Standing near a marble statue of a man, he asserts that there is no real difference between the statue and a living human being, because "you can make marble out of flesh and flesh out of marble". When challenged by D'Alembert, Diderot explains further what he meant: begin by pulverizing the statue until it is reduced to dust. Mix the dust with compost, water the mixture, and let it stand for a year or two, or a century, until it becomes earth. Plant seeds in this earth: peas, beans, cabbages. "The plants feed on the earth, and I feed on the plant", and thereby the dust of the former statue is transformed into flesh.

He continues his argument by reflecting on how nature, as it were, creates animals from nothing, by which he means that there is no prefiguring or intellectual design in their origin:

> Look at this egg: with it you can overthrow
> all the schools of theology and all the
> churches of the world. What is it? An
> insensitive mass, for the germ within it is
> merely inert, and thick fluid. How does
> it evolve into a new organization, into
> sensitivity, into life?

Diderot answers, "Through heat". And what causes heat? Motion.

He goes on, describing the process of germination and growth. First, there is a mere speck that moves about, an animate thread; the thread grows, thickens, takes on color and flesh, which forms itself into distinctive features: a beak, wings, eyes, feet, and internally, intestines and organs and bodily fluids, all covered over with down. The animate thing moves, breaks its shell, a bird emerges that walks, flies, feels pain, flees from danger, loves, desires, enjoys the presence of others.

And what of mankind? How does it emerge? In the very same manner. The human intellect, consciousness, and sense of being a person—or having moral worth—all in turn evolve. The mind is a wondrous system of filaments that function like a finely tuned lute. The vibrations of its strings can be controlled to fashion rare harmonies that play upon the mind, and evoke passions that are the beginnings of meaning.

THE AMERICANS

Establishing the Rule of Law

THE UNITED STATES OF AMERICA came into existence on July 4th, 1776 (or on a day very close to that), when delegates to the second Continental Congress adopted a resolution declaring that the original thirteen colonies were no longer colonies of Great Britain but "Free and Independent States", and that as such, they had "full Power to levy War, conclude Peace, contract Alliances, establish Commerce, and to do all other Acts and Things which Independent States may of right do".

This was the conclusion of the Declaration of Independence. But it was only the beginning, for the thirteen colonies, now, by their own declaration, independent states intended to stay together. Unity among them was deemed necessary, for none of them alone had power enough to defend itself against their former sovereign, Great Britain, with all its military might and power. It was clear that the British government was not about to let any of them go.

The Continental Congress continued to meet, and, two years later, on July 9th, 1778, it voted to form a confederacy, "a perpetual Union", to be named "The United States of America". To this end Congress enacted Articles of Confederation. By these articles, each state committed itself to mutual friendship and assistance, and the citizens of one state became citizens of them all, with all rights and immunities. Paramount authority was given to Congress ("The United States in Congress Assembled") to wage war and make peace, enter into treaties with foreign powers, and to regulate commerce and create currency. A common treasury was created, as well as a standing executive committee (the Committee of the States) consisting of one member from each state, which would carry on the business of government. However, neither the Congress nor the Committee of the States was empowered to act in any of these ways without the consent a super majority of nine of the thirteen states. No standing army or navy was established. Assembling militias and building warships remained the responsibility of each state; in time of war, Congress was empowered to requisition them and to appoint a commander-in-chief to lead them.

These arrangements proved sufficient to allow the United States to wage war successfully against Great Britain and gain its independence. In 1783, the Treaty of Paris was signed, which ended the war and granted the United States territorial rights to an area bounded by the Mississippi on the West, Canada on the North, and Florida on the South.

But, despite this victory, the United States remained a mere collection of states, each jealous of its freedom and independence—obsessed with self-interest, willful, irrational, and each with its own militia. What seemed to be irresolvable conflicts continually arose within and among them. For example, the question of slavery. And there was no national agency with power enough to establish and maintain peace.

It soon became clear to some cool heads that if the United States of America was to endure, it was necessary to find a more durable legal way to make them into an indivisible nation, to form a "more perfect union". To accomplish this, it was necessary to begin at the beginning, to rely on an authority that was prior to or more fundamental than the states and their constitutions. Taking a page from Locke, the founders looked to the people, and fashioned the notion of "the People of the United States", whose sovereignty they regarded as more fundamental than the sovereignty of any individual state. It was concluded that United States of America could become one nation only by the authority of the People, and that this must be accomplished by creating and adopting a constitution, one that did not depend merely on a consensus of delegations from the states but was "ordained and established" by the People.

It is important to recognize that the Constitution presents itself as a public declaration, with a voice, the people's voice that addresses the world in its magnificent preamble, which states its action and clarifies its purposes:

> We, the People of the United States, in
> Order to form a more perfect Union,
> establish Justice, insure domestic
> Tranquility, provide for the common
> Defense, promote the general Welfare,

and secure the Blessings of Liberty to
ourselves and our Posterity, do ordain and
establish this Constitution for the United
States of America.

And in Article VI, it is declared that this constitution would be fundamental law, the supreme law of the land, with which all laws and treaties, as well as all judicial decisions, if they are to count as law, must be consistent. Also, in Article VI, it was directed that all officeholders of the legislative, executive, or judicial branches of government, either of the states or the nation, shall be bound by oath "to preserve, protect, and defend" the Constitution.

There is an essential difference between the Articles of Confederation and the Constitution. The former is like a treaty between independent states, which claim particular sovereignty. The latter, which negates this claim, is more binding; it is an enactment by the People of a fundamental law. Indeed, it is presented as their original creation, as their primary will—it is noteworthy in this respect that, unlike the Declaration of Independence and the Articles of Confederation, there is no mention in the Constitution of a higher authority than the People, no references to divine providence. The Constitution is pure law and purely secular.

But who are "the People" credited with its creation? Remember that the United States was from the outset conceived as a republic rather than as a direct democracy. Madison maintained that the will of the people is the foundation of any true republic, but it is filtered through representatives who are, to be sure, popularly elected or, in the case of appointment of judges, selected in a public and open process.

So, is the notion of "the People" a fiction? Perhaps, yes, if one takes the expression literally. But, in another respect, no, because "the People" refers to something very real. Representatives are not private persons, but bearers of the people's will, which wills the public good. And sovereignty of the people transcends all other claims to sovereignty or presumed rights to exclusive power, whether that lesser sovereignty be wielded by a hereditary monarch, a tyrant, a dictator, a religious prophet, or the privileged few; it overrules them all. This is established by a fundamental law, the Constitution. Indeed, "We the People of the United States" means nothing without the Constitution of the United States. Together, they may be our surest defense against tyranny, the surest antidote to divisive factions and fractious conflicts, and an effective instrument—perhaps the only one yet designed—to secure for us and our posterity the blessings of liberty.

Power to "The People"

THE FRAMERS OF OUR CONSTITUTION, following John Locke, attributed sovereignty to the people. Yet the question remains "Who are the People?". Surely, this is more than a useful fiction or abstraction. "We the People" refers to actual people: those who directly or indirectly authorized the adoption and ratification of the Constitution, and who express their will by voting. But when this nation began not all the people dwelling in the land could do that, for women lived here and could not vote; also, slaves; and Native Americans, who were the original occupiers of the land. Only freeborn males counted according to that era's law: white, English, and mostly Protestant. They were "the people".

In *The Federalist no. 2*, Alexander Hamilton credits divine providence with having brought to this rich and fertile wilderness a united people: "a people descended from the same ancestors, speaking the same language, professing the same religion, attached to the same principles of government, very similar in their manners and customs, who... fighting side by side through a long and bloody war, have nobly established their general liberty and independence". Yet it was not until 1920 that women were granted the right to vote; the achievement of their full political and social equality remains unfinished business.

The 14th Amendment, which grants citizenship to all persons born or naturalized in the United States, along with all rights and privileges—guaranteeing equal protection by the laws—should have applied also to Native Americans residing in the states. Yet, their rights were not fully realized until 1924, with passage of the Indian Citizenship Act, which granted full citizenship to "non-citizen Indians born within the territorial limits of the United States". During the First World War, Native Americans who served in armed forces were granted citizenship. This act came as a consequence and in recognition of their service.

However, there was and remains a problem with regard to Native Americans. They were not immigrants to this land. Rather they were indigenous residents, and it was their land. Their ancestors were not nomadic transient dwellers, who never really occupied it, as is sometimes assumed. Nor was the territory of the United States a wilderness, when Europe began the colonization of America. There were Indian nations here before any of the states, and an international order. So, it is likely that the United States acquired this land by usurpation. These nations still exist, and, therefore, granting citizenship to their members, is, to say the least, an ambiguous act; it's like granting life to a living being. The Constitution does not explicitly recognize this fact, but there is recognition, in Section 1 of the 14th Amendment, that there may be persons residing in the states who are not under the jurisdiction of state or federal laws. The legal and moral issues involved are too great and complex to be examined here, but they cannot justly be ignored.

Slavery was abolished in 1865 by the adoption of the 13th Amendment. The 14th Amendment granted full rights and immunities of citizenship to all persons born or naturalized in the United States and required that representation in legislative bodies be apportioned according to "the whole number of persons in each state". Finally, in 1870, the 15th Amendment was ratified prescribing the right of all citizens to vote, regardless of their "race, color, or previous conditions of servitude".

Although there is reason to believe that these liberating measures might have come about in the course of time, and fear of their inevitability may have prompted the so-called Confederate States to secede, there is no doubt that their proximate cause was the American Civil War.

Which raises the question of the meaning of this terrible, cataclysmic event. According to law, it was an illegal rebellion and insurrection. The act of secession by eleven states violated the Constitution of the United States. By their vote to secede, the legislators of the seceding states became outlaws. Their waging war against the government of the United States was an act of treason. Viewed under the cool light of reason, secession was simply illegal. It may also have been a tragedy, and the figure who best represents this is Robert E. Lee. But

Lee was no hero. In any case, attempts to romanticize the Civil War are misguided, misleading, and unjust.

It is noteworthy that a leading argument of the Secessionists was that the government of the United States had turned tyrannical. They appealed to the law of nature, citing Locke to argue that the national government has the duty to protect the life, liberty, and property of the people. And that slaves are property—not people. In their view, the U.S. government's intention to abolish slavery was a violation of natural law and hence tyrannical. By their tyranny, tyrants forfeit their right to rule, and therefore, secession was justified. The argument is fanciful, but also odious.

But to return to my theme, almost a century more would pass before legislative measures were taken to guarantee equality of civil rights. In 1954, the Supreme Court declared segregation to be illegal, and a decade later the civil rights act was passed. And still the effort to establish freedom and equality for all continues; it was met with violent resistance, epitomized by the murder of Martin Luther King, Jr. And the violence continues.

Nevertheless, through all of this, "The People of the United States" has increased in substance, in reality. For that phrase has come to encompass not only white Protestant males, but all persons: male, female, black, brown, white, gay, lesbian, transgender, pious and freethinking. The trend towards diversity and inclusiveness continues. Because we can appeal to all of these persons to exercise their equal right and duty as citizens to vote, to raise their voices against injustice, to seek a redress for "grievances come", and to participate in the administration of justice—it is because of this, that "The People" is not a mere fiction or legal abstraction, but an unshakable foundation of freedom. "Power to the People", although under the rule of law.

Postscript:

Why has it been so difficult for us to achieve full equality? And why does the difficulty remain? The fault does not lie in the Constitution; it has been our only reliable means to achieve it. Rather it lies in ourselves. Human beings are just not very nice animals. They take comfort in their prejudices, and when the demands of justice seem inconvenient, they imagine themselves the victims of it. And they—or rather—we have an inexhaustible capacity to rationalize almost any unjust practice when it is in our personal interest. It is because of these facts that constitutionalism is our only reasonable mode of action in this time or any other.

The Reasonableness of the Constitution

To characterize something as reasonable, does not mean that it is delightful or pleasing. Eating ice cream or watching a movie may be delightful, but not necessarily reasonable if you are overweight. Having surgery is reasonable when it is necessary to save your life. Likewise with dieting, swallowing bitter medicine, exercising, and also morality and politics.

Madison may have borrowed from Locke the idea of the sovereignty of the people and used it to establish the authority of the Constitution. But he sided more with Machiavelli and Hobbes with regard the human character. He preferred their realism, shared their views of human nature, and agreed with them about the origin and nature of law and its necessity. These features of his thinking appear clearly in his writings in defense of the Constitution.

Begin with human nature: Madison agreed with Hobbes that a state of nature is a state of war of all against all, a lawless state, and that peace and civility would occur only if people covenanted together to form a civil society, and established a constitution, a fundamental law, as a means to this end. This system of government must be so designed "that its several constituent parts may, by their mutual relations, be the means of keeping each other in their proper places". And he went on to make this most memorable and quotable observation:

> But what is government but the greatest of all reflections on human nature? If men were angels, no government would be necessary. If angels were to govern men, neither external nor internal controls on government would be necessary. In framing a government which is to be administered by men over men, the great difficulty lies in this: you must enable the government to control the governed; and in the next place oblige it to control itself.
> [*The Federalist no. 51*]

A principal means of government self-control is the separation of powers. The power of government is divided into three branches: Legislative, which makes the laws, Executive, which puts them into operation, and Judiciary, which interprets the laws and policies of the other two branches and has the power to decide on their constitutionality. No branch is to encroach upon another; rather each is to be separate and independent, with "a will of its own", jealous of its particular prerogatives, endowed by law with "separate and rival interests". These interests gain potency when they combine the personal with institutional. The constitutional rights and duties of the office are incarnate in the person who occupies it. Selfish motives are institutionalized, the vices of human nature become instruments of public legality, even public virtue, and the powers of government are corralled and directed to achieve a common good. This idea would seem perverse, if it were not resplendent in practical wisdom.

Elsewhere, in *The Federalist no. 10*, Madison offers a similar defense of the Constitution. He laments that civil societies tend to fragment into factions or communities joined together and driven by a common impulse or passion or interest, which are opposed to the rights of other groups and to the common good. These special interests may be derived from religious, social, political, or economic motives: evangelical zeal, the ambition of aspiring politicians, partisan self-interest, identity politics, or the conflicting interests of rich and poor, of creditors and debtors.

The question is how to deal with this condition. One way would be to remove its causes. Factions are voluntary associations. What if individuals were prohibited from forming a faction? That would seem to be the most effective solution, for "Liberty is to faction, as air is to fire": remove the one, and the other will quickly die. But this would be sheer folly, if not suicidal, for just as air is essential to animal life, liberty is essential to political life. And political life is a necessity. In any case, as Locke proved, it is impossible to change beliefs by force or coercion.

Another way would be by creating unanimity of opinion and passion through universal education, to homogenize the people by indoctrinating them. But this is to assume that we can be certain that the opinions we propose to teach are true—this is a false assumption—or that human identities and their commitments can be changed at will. Besides, such an approach would subvert the very purpose of education, which is never to indoctrinate, but to foster a love of truth and a passion for free inquiry. Spinoza is right: freedom to seek the truth and follow it wherever it leads must never be abridged; to remain healthy, a republic requires a regular tonic of truth.

Besides, it would seem that the causes of faction are inherent in human nature. Human nature may be sociable, but human fallibility and selfishness and limited horizons more often cause us to prefer the society of others like ourselves, who share our prejudices. Factions, like evils, must come.

So long as a faction is a minority, the will of the majority should be sufficient to defeat its purposes if they threaten the common good. But what if a faction should grow into a majority? This is not an idle concern. If political parties count as factions, then, when one party controls all the branches of government, the possibility of tyranny of the majority becomes real, perhaps imminent.

Madison's response is that it is the very nature of the American republic to be armed to counteract this outcome. He did not conceive of our republic as a homogeneous city, but as an expanding union soon to embrace a continent. And although he did not use the term "diversity", he seems to have anticipated the necessity of it. The key was a combination of social diversity and a fundamental law, which provides that the branches of government and its institutions function competitively, and which subjects even the authority of "the People" to a rule of law that even they cannot revoke. Although they may amend it. This is the design of our nation: a nation established by fundamental law, the Constitution, which prescribes the separation of powers as a safeguard against tyranny and for the same reason requires that its officials in the legislative and executive branches hold tenure for a limited period, subject to the will of the people.

Will it work? One thing more is needed. Madison expected that over time a deep respect for law would take root in the minds of the people and the public officials who serve them, that reverence for the rule of law would possess the soul of the nation, and that our civil society would grow into a self-sustaining living thing. Madison hoped that the nation and its people would become virtuous. Was this a realistic hope?

The Irony of American History

THE TITLE OF THIS ESSAY IS BORROWED from a book published in 1952 by Reinhold Niebuhr (1892–1971), who is regarded as one of the outstanding intellectuals of the 20th century. He was a theologian, and a professor at Union Theological Seminary in the City of New York during its heyday. I take pride in having been one of his students, and although I no longer share his faith such as it was, I continue to find his views of human nature, history, and politics profound, powerful, and relevant, especially now.

I was reminded of Niebuhr's book while composing the previous essay in this collection. What could be more ironic than a constitution that relies on human selfishness to establish the rule of law? Besides, the title and theme of Niebuhr's book suggested a fitting way to conclude this series of essays on politics.

Irony is rooted in the ambiguity of meaning. For example, the versatility of language enables a speaker or writer to say one thing and mean just the opposite—or, even better, to mean both together, joining opposites in an implausible harmony. Take the famous line from Shakespeare's *Julius Caesar*, repeated by Mark Anthony in his funeral speech for Caesar: "For Brutus is an honorable man". Marcus Brutus worried over Caesar's ambition, and feared that he aspired to become tyrant of Rome, and so Brutus joined a conspiracy to assassinate Caesar. In all respects, he was an honorable man and was held in highest reputation, "the very best of the Romans". But the way in which Mark Anthony uses these words, the context and his tone of voice, means the opposite—or, to be precise, that Brutus' action shows that his noble character is flawed, conflicted, and capable of acting dishonorably. Mark Anthony's remark also reveals the ambiguity of the action itself and the character of the actors, for Caesar was murdered by honorable men, patriots all, who acted to save the republic. Which they ultimately failed to do. Shakespeare's *Julius Caesar* is a tragedy, and Brutus is its hero.

This is Niebuhr's point. Nations and their histories must be viewed through the filter of irony, which reveals the ambiguities of their noblest purposes, programs, and achievements. Only then do we understand them, grasp their essential meaning and assess their value. This is a hard and sobering truth, and even more, because it is a truth about all of us. Yet—and this is Niebuhr's other point—it is a truth that can save us, if we take it to heart. For such knowledge moderates our passion and causes us to be reflective and to pursue more modest goals.

The art of politics and the institutions that result from it are artificial things, designed neither by nature nor by God, but fashioned by human beings for their mutual benefit and convenience. Or, at least, this is their deliberate intention. Yet there is a tendency in our creative imaginations to overreach, to become overheated; to entertain utopian designs against all the evidence that reality or nature will not sustain them; to mistake our own motives and those of others; to believe ourselves to be wiser and more resourceful than we are; and finally to mix our noblest ambitions with personal pride, self-interest, private ambition, and, for good measure, no small amount of cowardliness.

Why does this happen not just once in a while, but too often, and most often when purity of motive and purpose are most loudly asserted? Niebuhr attributes it to a flaw in our nature. Of all the doctrines of Christianity, Niebuhr devoted most of his attention to the doctrine of original sin. According to this doctrine, sin originated with Adam, the progenitor of mankind, when he disobeyed God. According to the story in Genesis 3, God had forbidden him to eat of the Tree of the Knowledge of Good and Evil planted in the Garden of Eden. But Adam, prompted by Eve, who had been deceived by a serpent in turn, nevertheless disobeyed God and ate the fruit. As punishment, God deprived Adam and Eve and all generations after them of immortality and expelled them from Paradise. Life grew hard. Hobbes might have commented that this was the beginning of the war of all against all.

The doctrine is more finely developed in the New Testament. According to St. Paul, who doesn't mention Adam, sin is rooted in the vanity of the human imagination, in human pride and vainglory, in our fashioning God in our own image and worshipping instead of God this vain image; in short, reversing the order of things by worshipping the creature rather than the creator. As punishment, God imprisoned mankind in their own imaginations, willfulness, and narcissism, which may be something like being imprisoned in a realm of social media, Twitter, and Facebook—this dismal narrative is not as fanciful as it may seem.

The upshot of all of this, as St. Augustine put it, is that mankind has remained free only to sin, and, even though their minds sometimes catch a glimpse of the desired good, they are not free to do it, or at least not with a good will. Mankind is free to do evil, but not free to do good. Or, as St. Paul famously put it: "For the Good that I would, I do not, and the evil that I would not, that I do.... Oh, wretched man that I am". (Romans 7: 19, 24) Luther labeled this condition "the bondage of the will", and wrote a famous book about it in which he relies largely on St. Paul. Luther's thought is profound if one separates it from his theology.

Niebuhr's interest in this doctrine was precisely in the ambiguities of human agency that it revealed; in them he perceived the key to the meaning of human history. Because of this, although he consistently favored liberal social and political causes and was a strong and persistent advocate of them, he disavowed the ideals of liberalism and any belief in progress. He did not believe that it was possible for a nation through education and technology to achieve a perfect state, or even to come close to it—much less the world. Yet he was insistent that we should never cease to work towards this goal. Hence, while maintaining his firm stance of critical realism, he never allowed his pessimism to degenerate into cynicism, and neither did he abandon the struggle for social justice.

This must continue to be the goal of every American. And in this endeavor, the Constitution, our rule of law, with its checks and balances, should serve as our constant sword and shield, regulating our actions and clarifying our minds.

Postscript:

To follow this imperative requires that one be familiar with the Constitution, which is not difficult. It is short. Copies of it are easy to find, inexpensive, and convenient to carry around. They should always be handy. Consult your local bookstore.

· · ·

Suggestions for Further Reading

About the Author

Suggestions for Further Reading

I WAS MOTIVATED TO WRITE THESE ESSAYS by the conviction that the best way to prepare oneself for citizenship is to study the European political tradition in which our American system of government is embedded. At best, these essays are only an introduction to that tradition. To study it, requires reading the key writings on which it is founded, for merely to read a history of that tradition, no matter how comprehensive, is like serving on a jury that must reach its verdict by hearing only the closing arguments of the competing attorneys without having heard the evidence and the cross-examination of witnesses. It is imperative: if you want to understand politics, read the texts!

Fortunately, one need not be a scholar to do this. All of the works treated in this book are available in competent, reliable translations and published in affordable editions. The three main series in which they appear are *Everyman's Library*, *Oxford World Classics*, and *Penguin Classics*. They are all paperbound and of modest size, so they easily fit in your pocket and are available for ready reading. These editions all come with introductions that set the stage for the work itself. One of the cardinal rules of reading classics is to read them in context. You can find more details by going online.

About the Author

Victor Nuovo was born and raised in New York City. As a graduate student he attended Union Theological Seminary and Columbia University, receiving his Ph.D. from Columbia in 1964. In 1962 Victor joined the faculty of Middlebury College, Middlebury, Vermont, and first taught religion and then philosophy, becoming chair of the department. He retired from Middlebury in 1994 as Charles A. Dana Professor of Philosophy Emeritus. In 1996 he was appointed Visiting Fellow at Harris Manchester College, Oxford, and reappointed the following year as a Senior Research Fellow, a position he still holds. Victor's area of specialty is the history of philosophy, in particular, 17th century English philosophy. He has published six books about the English philosopher John Locke, most recently, *John Locke: The Philosopher as Christian Virtuoso* (Oxford University Press).

In 2006 he was elected to the Town of Middlebury's select board and served on the board for more than ten years.

Victor has been married since 1953 to Betty Nuovo, a former Vermont State Representative. They have two sons and four grandchildren and reside in Middlebury, Vermont.

www.ingramcontent.com/pod-product-compliance
Lightning Source LLC
Chambersburg PA
CBHW020123130526
44591CB00032B/390